T0194040

LIFETIMES
True Accounts
of Reincarnation

Frederick Lenz, Ph.D.

The Bobbs-Merrill Company, Inc.
Indianapolis   New York

Designed by Rita Muncie
Manufactured in the United States of America

Fourth Printing

Library of Congress Cataloging in Publication Data
Lenz, Frederick, 1950–
    Lifetimes: true accounts of reincarnation.
    Bibliography: p.
    1. Reincarnation—Case studies.   I. Title.
BL515.L46   133.9′013   78-11209
ISBN 978-1-9821-0227-2

With love and gratitude for Sri Chinmoy

With love and gratitude to Jackie Ostrowsky

ACKNOWLEDGMENTS

I would like to thank the following persons who have either directly or indirectly helped me with the preparation of this book: Professor Gerald B. Nelson, Ph.D.; Professor Charles Owen, Ph.D.; Professor Yakira Frank, Ph.D.; Professor Paul Dolan, Ph.D.; and Professor Jack Ludwig, Ph.D. I would also like to extend my gratitude to my father, Frederick P. Lenz, Jr., for his constant encouragement; to James Seligmann, my literary agent, for all of his thoughtful advice; and to Diane Giddis, my editor, who through her penetrating understanding and superb guidance has helped me transform the original manuscript into a much more humanistic book.

I would also like to thank Merv Griffin and Long John Nebel for awakening an early interest in me in things that lie

7

beyond the realm of sight. My continuing thanks go to Debby and Kevan for their patient proofreading, and to my typist, Nina France, for all of the work she always manages to get done when, as always, I present it to her at the last possible moment. Finally I would like to thank all of the persons who have allowed me to present their past life accounts in this book.

TABLE OF CONTENTS

Sri Krishna's Remembrance

Arjuna, you and I
Have passed through countless births.
I know them all,
Your memory fails you.
                    —Bhagavad-Gita, iv, 5.

INTRODUCTION

Our birth is but a sleep and a forgetting;
The Soul that rises with us, our life's Star,
Hath had elsewhere its setting,
And cometh from afar;
Not in entire forgetfulness,
And not in utter nakedness,
But trailing clouds of glory do we come
From God, who is our home.

William Wordsworth:
"Intimations of Immortality"

For most human beings the subject of death is associated with feelings of pain, loss, guilt and apprehension. These feelings seem to stem from a general lack of knowledge about what happens to a person after he has been declared clinically dead. During the past three years I have met and talked with one hundred and twenty-seven people who claim to know what lies beyond death. Their knowledge is founded on their personal experiences, which they related to me and which I have set down in this book. These experiences would be termed incredible or unbelievable by most people. But as we examine the accounts, we begin to see that there are a number of striking parallels among them, parallels that cannot be explained by coincidence or chance. Looking directly at the persons who have had these experiences, we find that they come from many different walks of life, religious persuasions, ethnic and geographic backgrounds. The one experience they all share is that each of them has remembered one or more of his past lifetimes on this earth.

It is not my purpose to either prove or disprove the theory of reincarnation. Instead I have sought to present the facts of the cases as I know them in the hope that the reader will be able to make his own determination. Before presenting the actual accounts, however, I would like to acquaint the reader with some of the circumstances that surrounded my study and the writing of this book.

I first became interested in the subject of reincarnation in the fall of 1969. That year I met two persons who claimed to have seen several of their past lifetimes. Normally I would have discounted any claims of this type as fanciful or hallucinatory. But both of the individuals who shared their experiences were well-known members of the academic community. I listened to their accounts with a skeptical interest, and while I was not completely convinced of the validity of their experiences, my curiosity was sufficiently aroused to prompt me to do some reading on the subject.

I read all of the available books on reincarnation. Through colleagues at the State University of New York who knew of my interest I was able to meet several more persons who remembered their past lives. I was struck by the fact that each of the persons who had experienced his past life encountered the same sequence of phenomena during his remembrance.

I began to keep a record of these accounts and of background information on the people who reported them. I wanted to know if any one type of person was more prone to having a past life remembrance than another. I also wanted to discover if past life remembrances occur more often to men or to women; if they are triggered by any particular type of phenomenon; if they occur more in one kind of environment than in another, and if the persons who claim to have had them were predisposed to a belief in reincarnation before their past life remembrance occurred.

Having collected a sizable amount of material which I considered of interest, I began to give lectures about reincarnation at colleges and universities across the United States and Canada. During the course of these lectures I discussed the overall theories of reincarnation and to a limited extent the cases I had studied. Several times after a lecture I was approached by members of the audience who had experienced a past life remembrance. I observed that the same phenomena that marked the earlier accounts continued to crop up in these new remembrances.

In 1975 I was invited to appear on several radio and television shows to discuss my research in reincarnation. On these shows I told how I had met a number of people who claimed to have seen their past lives, and I mentioned the specific times and places that these persons believed they had lived in their earlier incarnations. However, I did not discuss the parallel phenomena I had observed in these remembrances, except to say that I had noted similar features in all of the past life remembrances I had come across.

After these shows were aired I received letters and phone calls from other people who wanted to share their past life remembrances with me. I subsequently met with most of these individuals and recorded the details of their experiences. The same types of phenomena I had noted in the previous past life remembrances continued to occur in every new case I encountered. Since I had not discussed these either in my lectures or during my radio and television appearances, it would have been impossible for any individual to fabricate his account to make it similar to the others I had already been given.

In addition to the correlations between past life remembrances, I also noted that the experiences of the persons I interviewed followed the basic blueprint of the reincarnation process as it has been set down in *The Tibetan Book of the Dead* and other Far Eastern books on the subject of reincarnation. Only three of the persons I spoke with had read any of these books, and they had done so after their past life

remembrance had already occurred, in an attempt to understand more clearly what they had experienced.

From the one hundred and twenty-seven cases of past life
remembrances I have now collected, the following statistics
have emerged: (1) Seventy-four cases of past life remembrances occurred to women and fifty-three to men. (2) Ten
of these persons were under twenty-five; forty-seven were
between the ages of twenty-five and forty; forty-six were
between forty and fifty-five; and the remaining twenty-four
were over fifty-five. (3) Ninety-five of the cases have occurred to individuals who reside in the United States,
thirteen to people who live in Canada, and nineteen to
people who live in Great Britain. (4) Thirty of the persons
are professionals (doctors, lawyers, etc.); thirteen are blue-
collar workers; twenty-seven are housewives; thirteen work
in government jobs; fifteen are employed in agrarian and
farm-related professions; ten are students; and the remaining
nineteen either are self-employed (artists, writers, etc.) or are
unemployed. (5) One hundred and nineteen of the persons
I interviewed said that they had no belief in reincarnation
prior to their past life remembrance. Five of the remaining
eight said that they neither believed nor disbelieved in reincarnation; the three remaining individuals acknowledged
a belief in reincarnation prior to their remembrance.

At this point it might be helpful if I present the details of
my own background. I was born in San Diego, California.
When I was two years old, my parents moved to Connecticut,
where I spent most of my youth. I was raised in a Christian
home and attended public schools. As a child I loved to
swim, play with my friends, watch television and read. After
graduation from high school I traveled extensively through
the United States for a year.

Having completed my travels, I enrolled as a student at
the University of Connecticut. I received several scholar-
ships and in my senior year was elected to Phi Beta Kappa.
I graduated with high honors and was awarded a State of
New York Graduate Council Fellowship to continue my
education at the State University of New York at Stony

Brook, where I spent the next five years intensively studying English and philosophy and was awarded both my M.A. and Ph.D. degrees from the State University of New York. I am currently a university professor, teaching courses in Eastern philosophy at the New School for Social Research in New York City. I also give weekly lectures at Harvard, New York University and the State University of New York.

I personally have never had a past life remembrance. But during my interviews with people who have, I became aware of elements of their accounts that would be difficult to translate into any book. They spoke with awe, fear and wonder as they recounted their experiences to me. Although it is inevitable that my close association with these persons has provided me with a different perspective on reincarnation than the reader who is coming upon this material for the first time, I have tried to be impartial in editing and presenting the accounts in this book, seeking to report rather than interpret these experiences. I have deliberately avoided fitting them into neat formulas or categories that will enhance the conclusions I have drawn from them, but instead have placed them in categories which seem to be logically suggested by their contents, nature and origin.

Almost every person who reported a past life remembrance has requested that I not use his name for fear that unwanted publicity would do him or his family harm. I have respected these requests, and except for those few cases where an individual specifically gave me permission to use his name, I have omitted the last names of the people whose accounts appear here.

I am fully aware that my study has only scratched the surface of this subject, and I hope that others will follow the trail I have marked out with more complete and thorough studies of past life remembrances. I also hope that each person who reads this book will gain as much from it as I have gained from its preparation.

Frederick P. Lenz, Ph.D.
The New School for Social Research
September 13, 1978

LIFETIMES

THE REMEMBRANCE OF PAST LIVES

All goes onward and outward, nothing collapses,
And to die is different from what anyone supposed,
and luckier.

Walt Whitman
"Song of Myself"

For most people the remembrance of a past lifetime comes quite unexpectedly. As they are working, talking with a friend, dreaming, or engaging in some other daily activity, they suddenly find themselves witnessing scenes from a past lifetime. After the remembrance, which generally lasts from ten to twenty minutes, most persons are able to single out a specific factor which they believe triggered the experience. While they may have noticed this factor during their remembrance, it was only afterward that they made a conscious connection between that factor and the onset of their vision.

The most common factor seems to be a person's association with another person, place or object that in some way reminds him of one of his past lives. Remembrances also occur to some persons during their dreams or while they are praying or meditating. In some cases there seemed to be no particular factor that triggered the remembrance, or the factor was unknown.

In twenty-five cases people felt that visiting a city, town, or some other geographical location activated their remembrance. They reported that when they first arrived at the spot where their remembrance occurred, they had the feeling they had been there before. This feeling gradually increased in intensity until it precipitated their remembrance. Several persons told me they were drawn to the site of their remembrance by a subconscious urge. They had longed for many years to visit a particular country, city, or building without knowing why. But since their remembrance they feel as if they now understand why they were drawn to that particular spot.

Richard is a banker in London. A conservative gentleman who lives in the borough of Ealing, he was graduated from Cambridge and often returns there for weekend reunions with some of his former classmates. He is married and has one child. Throughout his life Richard has had a strong interest in medieval architecture. He gave little thought to the reason for his interest until he had an experience while on holiday in Salisbury. He and his wife had taken a train to Stonehenge, but when they arrived it was pouring rain. On an impulse they decided to stop and visit Salisbury Cathedral while waiting for the rain to stop. As he was walking inside the cathedral, Richard had the following remembrance:

> I arrived at the cathedral quite late in the afternoon,
> just before closing. The place was virtually empty,
> and I spent some minutes walking about, examining the
> architecture. The entire time I was there I had the most
> peculiar feeling that I had been there before, although
> this was my first visit. I stopped walking and glanced
> up at the arched ceiling of the cathedral. I was just about
> to glance back down when something caught my attention.
> The ceiling seemed to move, and then I was aware that I

was actually watching its shape change. The building was no longer complete; it was in the process of being built.

A flood of memories entered my mind. I came to know that I had been a laborer who had worked on the cathedral, helping to get it built. Memories of my wife and family who had lived in the town came to me. But the memories lasted for only a few minutes; then I found myself back in the present, as if nothing had happened at all.

In four cases the persons had experienced a remembrance of a place prior to visiting that spot. When they later came to that location, they immediately recognized it from their previous remembrance.

Jane had her past life vision while she was a high school student in San Diego. At that time her interests were divided among "boys, school and cheerleading." She did not fully understand the meaning of her remembrance until several years later, when she visited Greece and came to the spot she had "seen" years before.

It happened when I was just seventeen. I was at home, babysitting for my little sister. My parents had gone out to celebrate their wedding anniversary. I was in the kitchen cooking dinner when I heard a loud ringing sound in my head. It got louder and louder until I was very frightened. The sound did not come from outside me, but from within. The room began to shift and fade, and I thought I was going to pass out. The next thing I remember, I was standing on a cliff overlooking the sea. I was watching the waves roll in and break on the rocks far below me. I heard the pounding surf and smelled the salt air. I turned around and began to walk through a field that was behind me. The sun was out and I felt warm and happy. I was returning to my flock of sheep that I had left up at the pasture. As I walked I sang

a favorite song until I reached the crest of the hill. I
thought about many Greek towns that I would like to one
day visit. I sat down near the sheep and, all alone,
rocked back and forth singing. Then the vision ended,
and I was back in my kitchen.

I didn't know what to make of what happened to me,
and I figured that I had had some kind of vivid daydream.
However, several years later when I was on vacation
from college, I went to Europe, and one of the countries
I visited was Greece. I was very much attracted to some of
the small coastal cities. One day while motoring with
friends we came to a stretch of road that overlooked the
sea. I was filled with a number of conflicting emotions,
but one thing was clear: I wanted to get out of the car. I
asked my friends to stop for a minute; they pulled over
to the side of the road and I got out. I walked over to the
edge of the road overlooking the sea and looked down.
As I did I saw the exact scene I had seen several years
before in my vision in the kitchen. I turned around and
walked away from the car and my friends. I walked with
a purpose, as if I knew the way. I followed a path through
a field and began to ascend an embankment. When I
reached the top and looked around, I recognized the
spot where I had been with the sheep in my vision. It was
exactly as I had remembered it. I was filled with memories
of places and scenes, and I knew I had returned "home"
again. Although it made no sense, I felt that I had lived
there in another time. I returned to my friends in the
car and explained my sensations to them. They didn't
seem to understand what I was saying, and I finally gave
up trying to explain it to them.

Three remembrances were triggered by an individual's
visit to what he believed to be the site of his death in a former
lifetime. In these cases a person witnessed his death and
relived moments from it.

The following remembrance occurred to Alexis, a retired

businessman from South Carolina. All his life he had been
fascinated by the Civil War. When he was a child and
played war games, he always wanted to be the Confederate
soldier. Later on he pursued his interest by reading books
about the battles in the war. He was particularly fascinated
by the battle that took place in Gettysburg in July of 1863.

Alexis joined a Civil War Society that meets every week
in his town library. Each week a different member of the
society researches one particular event from that period of
American history and gives an oral report to the other club
members on his findings at the weekly meeting. Alexis chose
to give one of his reports on the battle of Gettysburg. He took
a trip to Gettysburg to do some research for his report and
had the following remembrance there:

I was visiting one of the battle scenes when I heard
shooting. I looked around and saw a number of men
in gray uniforms in the distance. They were advancing on
a squad of troops in blue. They formed a solid wall, and
I could hear them yelling and whooping as they
charged. The area was filled with cannon and rifle smoke.
I could hear the sounds of the cannons booming, smell
the acrid scent of the gunpowder, and hear the constant
firing of their rifles. Then I saw the two armies meet, and
they merged in the heat of battle.

My perspective changed from the spot I had been
watching from to the middle of the battle. I was lying
on the ground and my leg hurt awfully. I had been shot
in the leg and was bleeding. One of my friends was
ripping open my trouser leg, trying to get a look at the
wound. Suddenly I saw four soldiers in blue uniforms
coming over the rise. They took aim with their guns, and
before I could yell to my friend, they fired. My friend
fell to the ground and blood spattered all over his face. I
felt sick to my stomach and then very hot. Everything
buzzed and then the light faded. I found myself back
in the present.

Approximately one-third of the past life remembrances appear to have been induced by an individual's association with a person he believes he has known in a past life. However, in many of these cases the person who "recognized" someone from one of his past lives did not become fully aware of his previous association with that person when they first met. Many people reported that when they first met they felt as if they were encountering an old friend, but the full revelation of their past life association did not occur for several years.

Alison and John live in Boston, Massachusetts. They first met at a party in 1967. They felt inexplicably drawn to each other and soon fell in love. Both of them had a strong feeling that they had met before, although prior to their meeting their paths had never crossed. They were married a year later and moved into a small apartment in Cambridge. At the time of his remembrance John was in his third year of law school and Alison was working for the phone company as a service representative.

My wife and I had been married for several years
before we realized that we had been together before. One
night we were sitting in bed talking. As I looked at my
wife, I saw that the color of her hair was changing
from brown to blonde. Then the entire room changed.
Instead of being in our bedroom, I found that we were in
an entirely different room. There were tapestries on the
walls and thick fur rugs on the floor. The walls were
made of stone. My wife and I were dressed in clothes that
appeared to belong to medieval England. As I stared at
her in amazement, scenes of our past life together
appeared before my eyes. I saw that we were lovers, but
that our parents disapproved of our love. We were not
allowed to marry, and my wife was betrothed to someone
else. In despair she took poison and ended her own
life. I left England in a state of depression, never
wanting to return to my country again. I fought for

a time in the wars in the East. Eventually I returned to
a monastery and lived the rest of my life in seclusion. I
realized that we had been brought together in this life
to complete what we had not finished in our previous life
together. All this was shown to me in a matter of several
minutes. I saw everything in full pictures; it was like
I was watching a movie.

In almost all the cases of past life association I encountered, both people recognized that they had known each
other in an earlier lifetime, but this revelation did not always
occur at the same moment. Often the remembrance of one
person released similar memories in the other individual.
This was the case with Mary and Alice, two college teachers
who live on Long Island. Mary first met Alice at a faculty
party. She immediately had the feeling that she knew her
and tried to recall where they had met. She invited Alice to
come to her house several days later.

After we had eaten lunch we began to chat. Alice
told me quite a large portion of her life story. She had
a great many emotional and financial problems. As she
told me her problems I felt maternal feelings stirring
within me. I offered her advice to help overcome her
difficulties, and she took my advice, very much in the
way a child would accept instruction from a parent. Then,
as we were sitting in my kitchen, I had a vision. I saw the
two of us sitting in another room. I was no longer aware
of my kitchen or even of who I was. I had become
someone else, or I guess you might say I was me in a
different time. My friend was sitting across from me. She
and I were both wearing the clothing of Catholic nuns.
We were sitting in a small stone room with only one
small cot that had a crucifix over it and a wooden chest of
drawers against one wall. I was a Mother Superior and
the girl sitting in front of me was one of my novices.
She was having many problems and difficulties adjusting

to the religious life. I was advising her, and as I did I felt
a tremendous warmth for this young girl.

The scene changed. I saw her leaving the convent.
She was leaving with a young man whom she had known
before she entered the convent. She had decided not
to take her final vows. She tearfully said goodbye to me
and hugged me. Then she and her young man went off
together. I felt both happy and sorry for her. I was
happy that she had the courage to leave now, but I was
sad that she was not fulfilling her higher calling.

The vision faded and my new friend was sitting next to
me just as she had been in our past life in the convent. I
felt the same sweet feelings for her that I had in our
previous relationship in a former life. I was happy that
we had been reunited. I told her about my experience, but
I did not tell her of the location of the convent, which
I had seen was in a small town in southern France. She
told me that ever since she was a child she had wanted to
be a nun. I asked her if she had any idea where the two
of us had been together in the past life I had just
described to her. She said she thought it had been in
southern France. She then paused for a minute and
closed her eyes. Finally she told me the name of the town.
It was the same town that I felt we had lived in together.

Nine remembrances occurred when a person heard a piece
of music, saw a painting, or came into contact with some
object which reminded him of one of his past lives. Elizabeth
Lok is a writer who lives with her two children in a suburb
of Ottawa, Canada. In April of 1977, on a visit to New
York City, she related the following experience to me:

I was waiting to go out one evening, and while I waited
I decided to put on a record and relax and listen to
music. The music happened to be *Madame of Devia*,
which is extremely dramatic Spanish music. I was sitting
there listening when I suddenly discovered that the room

had completely changed. In a flash I had a different
vantage point; I seemed to be floating close to the ceiling
in a much larger room, which appeared to be the drawing
room of an eighteenth-century Spanish home. There was
an enormous fireplace on top of which were some sheaths
and crossed swords; there were oriental rugs on the floor,
and large dark leather hardwood Spanish furniture. I
looked around the room. On the mantelpiece over the
fireplace there was a band of wood in which a motto was
carved. And while I knew what the motto was, part of
me actually refused to read it. The people in the room
were gentlemen who were relatives of mine. They were
men of various ages dressed in black with white shirts. The
time, I would say, was evening; I think there was a fire
burning in the fireplace. The gentlemen were talking
together in a group by the fireplace. I would assume that
they had had dinner and they'd come in to have their
smoke and their gentlemen's chat. I recognized with
surprise that I was related to them and that they were
discussing me. And from my position up near the ceiling, I
thought of making myself known to them; then I thought,
"No. They were related to me, but this is not really me
anymore." About this time there was some kind of
interruption from the room in which my body was sitting,
and I found myself back in the body.

Victor is a commercial artist who lives alone in Los
Angeles. When he was a student at the University of California, he saw a photograph of a temple that was built on the
Inland Sea in Japan. As he looked at the photograph, he was
flooded with memories of another life.

I was doing a project in college on Japanese brush
painting. I had taken out a bunch of books from the
college library and was leafing through them in my
apartment. One of the pictures especially caught my eye.
It was a photograph of a temple that was built on platforms

on a lake in Japan. When I saw the photo, I knew that
I had been there before. I could see whole scenes inside
the temple. I could remember what the different rooms
looked like, and I even recalled people I had known there.
Several years later, when I was in the army, I visited
Japan. One of the many temples I visited was the one
I had seen years before in the art book. The temple guide
who conducted the tour was astonished because I was
able to tell him what was in each room before we entered
it, even though he knew that this was my first visit to the
temple. There could be no other explanation for my
experience except that I must have visited it in some
other life.

Remembrance Through Dreams

Nineteen people I spoke with had past life remembrances
while they were dreaming. After assessing their dream remembrances, I have been able to note four ways in which
these differ from ordinary dreams: (1) The dream remembrance was accompanied by sensations completely unlike
those they have experienced in any other dream; (2) during
the dream remembrance, they were aware that they were
seeing one or more of their past lives; (3) unlike most
dreams, which normally fade after several hours or months,
dream remembrances are so vivid the dreamer can describe
even the slightest details of his dream years later; and (4)
after someone has had a remembrance dream, he changes
his attitudes toward death and dying.

The sensations that accompany a dream remembrance are
similar to those that accompany a waking remembrance. In
both cases a person feels that all of his perceptions are crystal
clear and extremely vivid. These perceptions are accompanied by a feeling of joyous abandonment and ecstasy. A
young woman remembers:

During my dream remembrance I was in a state of
supreme ecstasy. The feelings that I had were different

from anything I have ever felt in a dream before or since. I have never known such a state of perfect love and joy; never have I experienced such rapture.

Pamela Cohen, a hospital worker who lives in Montreal, has had several past life remembrances, all of which occurred to her in dreams. In the following description she asserts that during her experience she was completely conscious of the fact that she was having a vision of one of her past lives.

I saw my past life in Kentucky in a dream I had several years ago. I saw that I was in the Old South. The roads were all muddy, and I had to pick my skirts up to walk across the street. As I was walking across the street, I could hear the noises of the wheels on the wagons turning, smell the horses, feel the heat of the day. I started off the dream looking at my feet in the mud, and I picked up my blue skirts and walked across the street to the stairs for the sidewalk. Instead of having steps that went straight up, you had to enter them from the side. Then I walked into the general store, and as I walked in I was totally at home. It was like breathing a breath of relief. There were other people in the store, but they didn't mean anything to me. I had the feeling that my life was very hard and drab. Coming to the general store was very exciting. I bought some red thread and calico material for a dress. I almost bought a blue ribbon for my hair, but I knew that I shouldn't spend that much money.

I knew this was not an ordinary dream. While I was experiencing all of this, there was such an intense feeling of familiarity about it all. It was like, "Oh, I'm home again! I haven't seen this place for so long! I know this place!" It was that feeling. It was so strong that there was no question. I had returned to a place where I hadn't been in a long time. This was a place that had been dear to me, that I had done a lot of shopping in.

I woke up right after it ended. This one and the other dreams of my past lives are much clearer and more vivid than my regular dreams. They always tell me things that help me understand certain feelings I have about things. Normally when I dream I'm not aware that I am dreaming. It's something I'm caught up in. But in these dreams I was fully aware the whole time that I was seeing into my past.

Persons who recounted their dream remembrances to me were able to do so in total detail. Unlike most dreams, which fade after a person has been awake for an hour or two, dream remembrances remain vivid for many years. Dream remembrances can also provide an individual with information that he feels helps him overcome problems in his present life. The following dream remembrance occurred to the owner of a foreign-car garage in Jacksonville, Florida. Since his youth he had been afraid of the water and had always avoided swimming and boating. But after his remembrance he claims to have understood and overcome his fear.

I was on a boat headed out to sea. The boat was small, and the wood on the decks was well weathered. I had left my home and headed down the coast in my boat to trade with the savages. The weather was good the day we left, and we had her under full sail. It was hot, and I enjoyed feeling the breeze strike my face while I stood on the bow. On the third day out from port the weather changed. The sky grew dark and was filled with black storm clouds. The wind picked up, and the rain began to fall in sheets. The groundswells doubled in size. The wind whipped the boat back and forth like a toy. I heard a terrible sound as the boat smashed into something. Water was rushing everywhere. I tried to swim, but my legs got tangled in a line. I was pulled under the boat and drowned. . . . I have always been afraid of the

sea and boats as long as I can think back. My dream
showed me why. I can understand my fear of them now,
and I am no longer as afraid as I was.

One of the most startling types of dream remembrances
is that in which the dreamer speaks audibly in a foreign
language of which he has had no previous knowledge in this
lifetime. If one is skeptical about the validity of dream remembrances, experiences similar to the following offer one
of the best possible arguments that a person in the dreaming
state is capable of seeing a portion of a past lifetime.

Lynn is a housewife who lives with her husband and
daughter in a modern development in Evanston, Illinois. Her
husband Roger works for a large bank in Chicago. One night
she and her husband were awakened from sleep by the sound
of a strange voice coming from their daughter's room.

> We got out of bed and went into her room but found
> her sleeping quietly. We were puzzled and were about to
> return to our own room when she began to talk in her
> sleep. She spoke rapidly in French in an unfamiliar voice.
> My daughter is only six and has never been outside this
> country and has never been exposed to anyone who
> speaks French.
> She spoke in French for several nights in a row.
> Neither I nor my husband has ever had more than an
> elementary course in French in college, so we had trouble
> following what she was saying. My husband borrowed
> a portable tape recorder from his office, and we made a
> recording of one of her conversations. We brought the
> recording to the French teacher at our local high school.
> She listened to it and told us that the little girl (our
> daughter) on the tape was looking for her mother, who
> she had been separated from when her village was
> attacked by the Germans. She said the little girl seemed to
> be lost and, judging from her tone of voice, was very
> distressed. It is my feeling that our daughter lived before

in a village in France and probably died in one of the
world wars.

Prayer and Meditation Remembrances

The seventeen prayer and meditation remembrances reported to me do not appear to differ in content from other
types of remembrances. There is a difference, however, in
the reaction of persons who have had remembrances during
periods of prayer and meditation in that these individuals
appear to accept their remembrances more readily than the
other persons I have spoken with. This can possibly be
attributed to the fact that they have already become accustomed to nonphysical phenomena and therefore do not
find it so difficult to accept their past life remembrance as
real.

Joan is thirty-four years old and lives in San Diego, California. Because she works for an advertising agency and is
under a great deal of pressure most of the time, she started
to meditate in the hope of overcoming stress and worry. She
usually meditates for a half hour in the morning before she
goes jogging and again for a half hour in the evening after
work. One evening she had the following remembrance:

I was on the porch meditating when I noticed something
unusual happening. Usually when I meditate I feel
very peaceful. That evening my meditation was different.
I started to see all kinds of colors—colors I had never
seen before. Images began to dance and swirl in front of
me. Then they began to form scenes and pictures. At first
they were indistinct, and I could vaguely see people
moving about; then they slowly came into focus, and
everything became crystal clear.

I saw a woman seated on a long couch. She looked to
me to be about seventy years old. She seemed to be alone;
at least I was not aware of anyone else's presence. When
I looked at her I knew I was looking at myself in another

lifetime. Small memories began to filter into my mind from that life. I remembered my wedding, my children, my husband's death. Then the scene faded and another appeared. I was on a beach, and there were two children, a boy and a girl, playing in the sand. The girl was wearing a red print skirt and her hair was tied into braids. Again I had the feeling that I was looking at myself; this time it was in a different life from the one I had seen before. Memories and feelings came to me again. I thought of my parents, my home—simple childlike thoughts. This scene faded and another appeared. . . . During the course of my experience I saw six or seven different lifetimes. Each one gave me a brief glimpse of something I had been before. Each one showed me something intimate and special about myself.

Spontaneous Remembrances

Ten of the cases of past life remembrance appear to have occurred spontaneously—that is, the persons to whom these remembrances occurred could not locate any physical or psychological stimulus that set them off. It is possible, however, that these remembrances were triggered by some association or stimulus that the individual was not conscious of.

The following spontaneous remembrance occurred to Tom, a man in his late fifties. He lives in a small town in eastern Connecticut, where he is the only doctor and does everything from treating colds to delivering babies. He had the remembrance in the fall of 1975, but his experience seemed so incongruous that he was reluctant to tell anyone about it. One evening he heard me discussing reincarnation on the Long John Nebel show, and the next day he sent me a letter describing his experience. I subsequently met with him, and he gave me the following account:

One day in late October I was outside in my yard raking leaves. I had been working hard all morning, and I felt it was time for a break. I sat down under a maple tree and was starting to relax when my whole body began to shake violently. I lost awareness of where I was, and all I could see was blackness in all directions. I felt I was plunging down a long black tunnel; I was nauseated from the falling. Then I began to see light at the end of the tunnel. I found myself sitting upright in a chair in my living room. One of my servants approached me and told me that my horse was ready for my trip into town. I followed him outside the house, mounted my horse, and rode into town. I remember that I passed a group of merchants on camels on the way to town. They were all acquaintances of mine, and each one paused for a moment of brief conversation. We discussed the weather and the state of the crops. After each encounter, I continued my journey toward the town. Arriving in town, I dismounted and entered a drinking house. There I joined several of my friends and we drank and joked for some time. The thing that stands out in my mind the most was how real everything was. I could see the crowds of people inside, feel the metal goblet in my hands, and taste the drink. I even was sexually aroused by seeing some of the women there.

A fight broke out, and there was yelling and cursing. I was thrown violently to the floor. Before I could raise myself up I was kicked in the head, and I lost consciousness. I found myself surrounded by blackness again. . . . I found I had returned to the present. I was sitting up straight under the maple tree in my backyard.

Another case of a spontaneous remembrance involves Allen, a mechanic who lives in Eugene, Oregon. A veteran of Vietnam, Allen had been married for two years before he and his wife divorced. One of his favorite pastimes is hiking. One afternoon in late fall he and a friend were climbing a small mountain outside of Eugene. During one of their rest periods he had the following remembrance:

I found myself in a very dark room. There were six
or seven men clustered around me talking quietly. They
were dressed in dark-colored robes. They were priests
of ancient Egypt and had just initiated me into their
priesthood.

The next thing I knew, the room vanished and I was
standing on top of a sacrificial altar. A naked young
girl was lying before me. I sensed that I was much older
now. I had a long knife in my hand. It was my function
as the high priest to offer this girl in ritual sacrifice.
The crowd below me waited in silence. The girl's face was
soft and her eyes were glazed. I knew that she was not
struggling as a normal person would because they had
drugged her before she was brought out that day.
This was done so that the common people would believe
that she was willingly going to her death. The vision
shifted. Now I was looking into the eyes of another man.
His eyes blazed like two fires. He was my occult teacher.
As I watched him, his whole body seemed to shimmer
before me. He placed one hand on my forehead, and as he
did a thrill ran through my body. He was instructing
me in magical practices.

A woman's face swims before my eyes. She is wearing
a tall conical hat. She is my wife. We live in a palace.
There is a plague upon the land. She is the most beautiful
woman I have ever seen in my life. Her skin is pale
and clear. She has traced dark outlines with makeup to
elongate her eyebrows. I am consumed by her totally. I
think of nothing but her. She is distant and cold, like a
cat. I would stay with her, but I must go to talk with the
officials. She gazes at me as I leave, unconcerned but
totally aware. I feel that she is almost unhuman. Yet I am
totally devoted to her. She has given me two sons.
She waves as I depart. As she slowly turns around, her
white gown gently moves in the wind. It touches the floor
ever so slightly as she walks. I leave her.

I have always been attracted to Egypt. Whenever

I visit a museum I find myself automatically walking to
the Egyptian displays. When I visited the British Museum
in London I was totally fascinated by the displays of the
Egyptian jewelry there. The Egypt I remembered was
quite different from the one we read about. There was
another Egyptian civilization that was much more
mystically oriented prior to the Egyptian civilization
we see relics of. Most of it was destroyed in terrible wars.
I have seen some of this in full pictures. The rest I just
have come to know. It was as if I had amnesia, and after
my past life visions I just started to remember things I
had forgotten.

Returning

Most people reported that their remembrance terminated
without any special circumstances. At a certain point in their
experience their visions began to fade and then stopped
completely. But twenty-nine persons said that they experienced a particular sequence of events at the end of their
remembrance. In these cases the individual passed through
"a long black tunnel" at the end of which was a "bright white
light." After passing through the tunnel, he regained his
physical awareness, and his remembrance faded.

At the end of Allen's Egyptian remembrance he experienced the phenomenon of returning. The people and places
in his vision became less clear to him. For a short time he
was unable to see anything but blackness, and he felt he
was passing down a tunnel.

The way down the tunnel was long and dark. I was
brought along without being aware of where I was
going. I saw a bright white light at the end of the tunnel.
It grew brighter and brighter as I got closer to it. It got
so bright that it was blinding. The next thing I knew I
was back on the mountain as if nothing had ever happened
to me. Everything around me seemed to glow and

sparkle like it does after it rains. I felt great. The world
seemed new and I felt new. I felt like I had been reborn.

In three of the cases a person's remembrance was interrupted by an external stimulus. In one instance it was the
sound of a telephone ringing, and in the other cases it was
the sound of someone's voice. There seem to have been no
negative effects from these premature interruptions, although
all three persons had a vague feeling that more would have
been revealed to them if the interruption hadn't occurred. A
woman remembers:

> I heard a voice in the distance. It was calling my name.
> It was so insistent, it wouldn't leave me alone. I opened
> my eyes and saw my husband. He told me that we had
> arrived at my mother's. It seemed absurd that we were
> still in the car. I must admit I resented him for calling
> me back. He sensed I was upset and asked if I was all right.
> I started to tell him about it, but I stopped; he wouldn't
> have understood. I felt I would have learned much more
> if he hadn't called me back.

Perception of Time

After the termination of their remembrance, most people
were surprised to discover that the entire experience had
lasted only ten or twenty minutes; they felt that it had gone
on for several hours or even days. Others felt that they had
gone beyond time to a state of existence in which earthly conceptions of time had no meaning. In either case they were
amazed to discover they had experienced so much in such a
brief span of time.

A construction worker from Indianapolis, Indiana, states:

> It seemed incredible to me that only five or so minutes
> had passed. I felt that I had been away for days or
> weeks. I stared at my watch in disbelief. My first reaction

was that I had better see what was wrong with my watch. Then I checked the clock in the kitchen and discovered that there was nothing wrong with my watch.

After Mary viewed her past life in the convent with Alice, she saw two more of her past lives. Reflecting on her remembrance, she remarked that throughout her experience she was never conscious of the passage of time. In the following segment of her account she explains her perceptions of time:

I went to a place where there was no time. I was beyond birth and death. Nothing on earth mattered there. I was in the middle of eternity. I felt that a part of me had always been there. When I came back and looked at my watch, it all seemed so absurd. I watched the second hand of my watch moving around the dial. But I was not connected with it. I could still feel a part of me out there in eternity. How could I ever be concerned about time and death when I had seen that my soul would always live in eternity? I had to laugh at how silly I had been for so many years to be worried about time. I had all the time in eternity at my disposal. At the same moment I also had another feeling. Time was something to be used.

THE EXPERIENCE OF REINCARNATION

To see a World in a Grain of Sand
And a Heaven in a Wild Flower
Hold Infinity in the palm of your hand
And Eternity in an hour.
           William Blake:
               "Auguries of Innocence"

From the one hundred and twenty-seven interviews I conducted, I have been able to formulate a model for the typical past life remembrance. While it does not represent all possible phenomena that a person can experience during a past life remembrance, it does include those experiences that most of my interviewees have had.

A man is engaged in normal activity when he hears a high-pitched ringing sound. The sound grows in intensity until it blocks out all other sounds in the room. He feels his body becoming very light, as if it is floating in the air. His surroundings start to grow hazy, and he sees many different-colored lights passing before his eyes. The entire room starts to vibrate; he sees patterns formed by these vibrations in the air and the objects around him. He loses sight of his physical surroundings and feels that he has gone beyond his body.

He begins to feel ecstatic. He is filled with such a profound sense of well-being that he does not worry about or question what is happening to him. He discovers that he has stopped thinking, but finds that he can understand things without having to think. He is totally conscious of everything that is happening to him; he feels that he has never been more conscious of anything in his life.

A variety of different scenes and events flash rapidly before his eyes. Each scene is suspended in time, and his momentary glance allows him to experience every part of it. He feels that he is watching a play or a movie. He can see people, hear their conversations; and he gradually becomes aware that the scenes and the people are from one of his past lives.

After realizing that they directly concern him, he watches the scenes more intently. Soon he can distinguish one particular character in the "movie" whom he recognizes as himself in a previous life. He does not see every aspect of his former life; he sees only parts of it.

His awareness changes, and he finds that instead of just watching the "movie" of his former life, he is now actually participating in it. He talks, feels sensations, smells odors, and completely relives moments from his past. His consciousness alternates: some moments he is aware that he is watching the "movie," and other moments he forgets that he is viewing a past life and becomes totally absorbed in experiencing it.

Eventually the visions begin to fade, and he starts to become aware of his physical body. Soon the visions stop and his experience comes to a close.

The preceding model does not include every possible variation in the phenomena I have encountered, but it does accurately reflect the outstanding features of most remembrances in the order in which they most frequently occur. The obvious similarity of these phenomena and the frequency with which they appear suggest that the persons who experienced them have neither imagined nor fabricated them. In the following pages I will explore these parallel phenomena in an attempt to better understand what they are and their

overall significance within the framework of a past life
remembrance.

The Sound

Interviewees reported that they first became aware they
were entering an altered state of consciousness when they
heard a high-pitched ringing sound. This sound became
louder and louder until it blocked out all other noises. At first
most people tried to determine whether the sound was coming from something around them. As it grew in intensity, they
realized that it was coming from within.

One person who reports such an experience is Harry, who
owns a small sporting goods store outside of Albany, New
York. In high school he was the star of the baseball team,
and after graduation he accepted an offer to play with a
major league team, playing for several seasons before he
retired from baseball to buy a store. He now lives with his
wife and three children in the suburbs of Albany. Harry's
remembrance, in which he saw his former life as a French
soldier, occurred one night in December of 1975:

> I was with my wife in the bedroom. It had been a
> normal day. The kids were in bed and I had just put on my
> bathrobe. I began to hear a ringing sound. I almost didn't
> notice it at first, but it kept getting louder and louder. I
> asked my wife if she knew where the sound was coming
> from. She told me she didn't hear anything. I told
> her I had a loud ringing sound in my ears. She told me to
> go to bed and forget it and that it would be gone in the
> morning. I was very upset. I went downstairs to the living
> room and turned on the TV. I thought that if I watched
> for a couple of minutes it might go away. The sound
> didn't leave me, though; it kept getting louder. It finally
> got so loud that I couldn't even hear the TV.

Leonard is a premed student at the University of Wisconsin in Madison. He spends an average of seven to nine hours

a day studying. One night he was studying in his apartment with his girlfriend, Susan, when he heard the sound.

> I was putting my books away and crunching up some papers before tossing them into the garbage can. Then I heard the noise. It started like a high-pitched sound; it was so high that I could barely hear it. Then I heard it shift in key. It was so loud that I thought something awful was happening to me. I was aware of nothing else. I didn't want to scare my girlfriend, so I tried to ignore it, but it didn't go away.

Feelings of Weightlessness

After the sound fades, a person begins to feel that his body is growing lighter. Many people said that they felt as if they were "floating on a cloud," "floating on water," or "falling." Harry told me that after the ringing sound subsided, his body began to feel very light.

> My body started to feel lighter. It was the same feeling I experience when I go down very fast in an elevator.

Leonard recalls:

> I've had dreams where I floated off my bed; it was kind of like that. It didn't feel bad. I've had a similar sensation at the dentist's when he used laughing gas. My body was numb and weightless.

Seeing Colors

The majority of people I interviewed reported that they saw flashes of brilliant color at the onset of their remembrance. These colors seemed to fall into two groups: colors that we normally see, and those that do not appear in the physical world. Most people reported that the colors were always very beautiful and bright, and that they were organized in a progression of hues, similar in appearance to a rainbow. A number of people said that seeing the colors soothed them. But the aspects of the colors that were emphasized in most accounts were their "brilliance" and their "phosphorescence." Harry, for instance, reported:

> The colors were beautiful. I have never seen colors
> like them. Many of them were colors I had seen before, but
> I have never seen any that glowed so brightly. I forgot
> all about what was happening to me and just enjoyed them.

Leonard's description of the colors he saw was similar to Harry's, except that he emphasized their clarity.

> I had not seen most of the colors before. Each color
> was vivid. Everything that met my vision was crystal
> clear and sharp.

When Alexis was at Gettysburg, he was literally overcome by the beauty of the colors he saw in the early stages of his remembrance.

> I kept seeing these bright bursts of color. They were
> mostly in the blue and gold range. I watched the colors
> move and shimmer. How could I describe it except to say
> that they were the most beautiful colors I had ever seen?
> My body was bathed in their light.

Vibrations

The next major change in perception is that everything around the person begins to vibrate. These vibrations can be seen, felt, and in some cases heard. Most people believed that these vibrations unlocked an inner door that led to the memories of their past lives. The following description is representative.

Allen felt that the experience of vibrations was the most remarkable previsionary part of his Egyptian remembrance. From his vantage point on the side of a mountain in Oregon he saw all of nature "vibrating in one motion."

All of life started to vibrate. I don't really think that it was starting to vibrate just for me, though; I think it must always vibrate like that, but I'm not usually aware of it. Everything around me started to move in rhythmic harmony. The trees, the grass, the sky, even my own body —everything that was in my sight was vibrating together. At first different objects seemed to vibrate at different rates of speed. Then I saw that they were all vibrating together; they were part of one overall movement.

Feelings of Well-Being

I have repeatedly asked people why they were not terrified by the extraordinary experiences they had during their re-membrance. Their response was that the feelings of joy and peace that accompanied them were so profound that they never questioned what was happening to them. Many people reported that they felt as if they were small children and their "parent" was guiding them through the experience. Others have associated these sensations with God or with some spiritual presence. Many individuals felt surrounded by love or complete joy.

Reflecting on his remembrance at Salisbury Cathedral, Richard recalls:

The only thing I can say is that the feelings I had all the way from the first moment to the last were so terrific that I never worried about it. Imagine if someone took you on a vacation and you were happier than you ever were before. Would you be upset that you were so happy? Would you ask someone to rescue you?

Harry explains the feelings he had during his remembrance in the following words:

> When I was a kid, my mother would sing to me while I
> fell asleep. That's how I felt. I forgot about all the
> hassles in my life. It was like I had never lived this life.
> I was in another world, and everything there was pure and
> beautiful. I really didn't want to come back.

Pamela Cohen remembers:

> I never wanted it to stop. All I could see was light, an
> ocean of white light. I was complete for the first time in
> my life. Every part of my being—my body, my mind,
> my feelings, my soul—felt like it was together.

Knowing Without Thinking

Saint John of the Cross and many other mystics have described a state of profound meditation in which they went beyond the borders of the physical world and entered into a spiritual realm of "pure knowledge." In this realm all things are preknown. Instead of their having to calculate a problem or question, the answer comes to the mind of the questioner before the question has been completely formed. This state, referred to as "No Mind" by zen masters, is experienced during certain phases of a past life remembrance.

The realizations which a person arrives at in this state of "knowing without thinking" are accompanied by the certainty that his knowledge is completely accurate. These realizations usually occur in the early stages of a remembrance, although a few individuals have reported "knowing without thinking" at different stages in their experiences. An individual feels that he has always known these things, but that he had somehow forgotten them. The most common realizations related to their understanding of the nature of existence and their purpose in life. Some people reported that they "knew" they were eternal; they sensed that a part of them had always existed and would always exist. Others became conscious that they had a soul and that their soul wanted them to have specific experiences and achieve different goals in each of their lifetimes. These perceptions often came very rapidly, sometimes several at a time. Most people told me that their new realizations stayed with them after their remembrance ended and helped them in many ways long after their experience was over.

During Joan's meditation remembrance in which she saw herself as an elderly woman, she feels that she came to "know" that she had a soul. She had been told that since she was a child, but the idea had always seemed vague and elusive to her. During her remembrance, this knowledge came to her in an intuitive flash. She felt it was a process more of remembering than of learning something new.

When I was a young girl, we would have religious instruction one afternoon a week. They used to tell us about the soul—how it lived forever and all that. I always believed what they told me; it made sense to me. I always thought of it as being a little tiny glowing thing. My ideas are changed now, to say the least! I saw my soul, and it was much bigger than I had ever thought. It wasn't something that I could say was so many feet long or so many feet high or anything like that. It wasn't a thing that was made out of matter. And it was so bright! It shone brighter than the sun ever could.

Harry's realizations had to do not with his soul but with his overall perceptions of life and its value.

The experience increased in intensity to the point where I didn't know if I could handle it. My mind had stopped thinking, and I felt like I was in another place where there was no time and no physical dimensions. I was still aware of what was going on around me, but at

the same time I was seeing another side of existence.
I knew more about life in those few minutes than from all
the perceptions and ideas that I had formulated during
an entire lifetime. I realized that every idea I had had
about myself and this world was wrong. It was all
perfectly clear to me now. Life no longer seemed drab.
I felt that it was an incredible gift just to be alive.

The Movie

After the experience of "knowing without thinking,"
images and scenes begin to appear before an individual. For
many people this experience is like watching a movie or a
play. They observe the actions of the "players," identify
themselves in the drama, and reflect on their actions. But
while they are viewing scenes from their past life, they are
unaffected by them. They feel as if they are viewing portions
of their past history the way a scientist would observe a
specimen under a microscope. In the following passage from
his interview, Allen describes his sensation of watching a
movie as he viewed scenes from his past life in Egypt.

Everything was composed of flickering images. As
my experience increased in intensity, the flickering images
began to become solid. I watched landscapes change,
buildings appear and disappear, and people pass in front
of me. The whole time I felt completely uninvolved.
Even though I had never had an experience like it before,
I felt totally unaffected by everything I was witnessing.

During some sections of John's medieval remembrance he
also had the feeling he was watching a movie.

The impression I had was that I was being shown
scenes from my past life for my own educational benefit.
My job was simply to watch the selected clippings of my
life and learn. At times it was like seeing a movie in

which I was the star. Sometimes I acted well, sometimes poorly.

Pamela Cohen remembers:

I can still vividly recall the scenes from my past life experience. I saw cities, castles and farms. I recognized people I knew that were related to me. I saw myself as a poor farmer's wife. The whole time I was watching all of this, I was bemused. I felt that I was watching a play about someone I vaguely knew. I saw hundreds of different scenes a minute. It was like watching a crazy slide show where the slides are shown so fast that you can hardly keep up with them. Yet I was able to look at each one and understand it completely.

Full Participation

Most of the people who reported past life remembrances to me described "full participation" in scenes and events: in this stage of the remembrance a person feels he actually experiences portions of it. He is able to taste food, hear conversations, smell odors, and feel pleasure and pain exactly as he did in his former life. Often he becomes so caught up in his experiences that he completely forgets his current life. However, many persons are able to relive their remembrance while aware that this experience is separate from their present life.

The phenomenon of "full participation" is one of the most difficult-to-grasp aspects of a remembrance for someone unfamiliar with the experience. The idea that a person can relive moments from his past is, however, in keeping with two experiences most of us have had. When we go to a play or a movie, there are times when we become so engrossed in what we are watching that we forget we are sitting in the audience and are able to share the experiences of the characters.

Another and even closer parallel can be drawn between the experience of full participation and dreaming. When we dream we are able to hear, taste, touch, think and feel emotions. Many times upon waking we are amazed when we discover that we were only dreaming. Full-participation experiences are far more complex than dreams and occur while a person is fully conscious, but the parallel may make it easier for us to understand the phenomenon.

Neil is a twenty-three-year-old divinity student who lives in San Francisco. One afternoon in April of 1975, while walking across a bridge, he had the following experience:

> I began to feel that my whole body was shaking. I looked up at the top of the bridge, but it was no longer metal. Only an old wooden bridge met my vision. I saw that I was wearing sandals and a long ochre-colored robe. I was carrying a wooden staff in one hand and I was slowly walking across the road.
>
> I felt I must be very old. My steps were very slow and steady. I paused partway across the bridge and looked out over the rice fields. I could see several families working together in the fields planting their crops and adjusting the gates of the water terraces that controlled the amount of water that entered their rice paddies. Several families passed me on the bridge, leading their oxen and carts. They bowed to me when they passed, for I was a monk. I bowed back, wishing each one inner and outer prosperity, and I strove to see the face of the divine Self in each person who walked past me.
>
> Standing on the bridge, I entered into a state of profound meditation. I felt that the waters that flowed beneath me also flowed within me. My physical body seemed to dissolve, and I felt the presence of the Supreme Self within the depths of my being. Eventually I returned to the monastery.
>
> My room was very small and simple. There was a mat for sleeping and a small wooden table for writing on which

were my pen and ink. A small table for meditation was set
in the eastern corner of my room near the window. From
the window I could see out into the meditation courtyard
and gardens, where many of the monks spent their days
absorbed in contemplation.

Other scenes from my life passed before my sight. I
saw my parents and my childhood in a small province in
the south of Japan. I witnessed my initiation as a young
monk by the Roshi. I saw my years of meditation in the
monastery, and I also saw myself leaving the monastery
and entering the world. I fell in love and lived with
a beautiful girl for several years. We lived by a river that
made melodious sounds as the currents drove the waters
upon the rocks near our small hut. I remembered the
nights we spent listening to the crickets, and the many sad
and happy moments we spent together. I witnessed
my wife's painful death and my own return to the
monastery. And then I realized that all the years I had
spent in meditation and teaching others the way of zen
since that time had been in preparation for this day. Today
was to be the day I would pass from this world into
the other world. The vision that I had on the bridge earlier
that day was a preparation for my death that was to come.

The vision faded and I found myself returned to
the present. I had somehow continued to walk during the
experience, and I was now approaching the end of the
bridge. I felt that I had been away for days, but it
had taken only a few fleeting seconds.

Five Less Frequently Reported Phenomena

There was remarkably little variation in the structure of
the remembrances recounted to me. However, I have observed that there are a number of phenomena that do not
appear in the majority of cases but have occurred often
enough to warrant their study. The five most common—the
"etheric body," the "silver thread," the "Guide," the "judg-

ment" and the "chain of lifetimes"—have been mentioned in at least twenty-five remembrances.

The Etheric Body

During a certain stage in a past life remembrance a person loses awareness of his physical body. While he is viewing or participating in scenes from a past life, he becomes conscious that he has another form. This form has been described as a "subtle body," a body made out of "ether," a "transparent form" and a "pure mind." The majority of people told me that although they were aware of it, they did not take any special notice of this subtle form because they were totally engrossed in the scenes from their past lives. But in over forty remembrances, individuals had such intense experiences in their "etheric body" that they were forced to become more conscious of its nature.

During their remembrance these persons first became aware of their etheric body when they felt it separating from their physical body. When this separation occurred, their conscious awareness "moved" from their physical body to their etheric body. Often at this point a person was able to look back at his physical body and see it in an entirely new way. Some reported that instead of seeing their physical body as they usually would, they saw it as a "broken toy" or a "dead, lifeless thing." Others, however, saw their physical body as a "shaft of light" or a "beautiful friend" whom they once had known but now felt removed from.

People describe their etheric body as being approximately the same size and shape as their physical body. They felt it was not composed of matter but of some light, translucent ethereal substance capable of traveling through both space and solid objects with equal ease. As they traveled from one location to another, they felt that they were passing through another dimension. Their etheric body moved by "flying" from one location to another, though they did not consciously direct its movements; it seemed programmed to take them to specific locations.

Marge works in a factory in Kansas City and is married to a sergeant in the army. Her father died when she was seven, and her mother was forced to go to work to support herself and her children. Marge had her remembrance one morning while she was getting ready to go to work.

I am a very nervous person. I find it difficult to relax in strange situations. When I first felt something happening to me, I was very scared; I tried to stop the feelings I had from happening. Almost in spite of myself they continued to grow stronger. I felt that I was in two places at once. I was inside of my mind and body, and at the same time I had the feeling that I was in another body. I know this sounds pretty strange, but it felt even stranger than I can tell you. Then I lost my physical mind and body. I could see them, though; I was up near the ceiling and I was looking down at myself. I saw that my eyes were closed and I looked like I was asleep. I hovered around my body for a time and then I went somewhere else. I wasn't physically moving; I wasn't walking. It was more like flying. I could feel my body; it was made of energy. The whole thing vibrated. I was completely relaxed. I was going from one place to another, and my body was taking me—I don't know how. It seemed to know the way. . . . At one point I remember looking at my body. It was the same shape as the physical body I had left before, only it glowed. I had the feeling that I could go anywhere I wanted to with this body, but I was satisfied to let it go and see where it would end up. Somehow I knew to let my body guide me, and I wasn't even nervous through any of it.

Before Leonard saw his vision of a previous lifetime, he "traveled" in his etheric body. During this segment of his remembrance he felt that he was traveling not through space but through another dimension.

I was moving through a dark tunnel, and then I saw
the sky. It was nighttime. The stars were above me; they
were clear and beautiful. I was in my body, but my body
wasn't made of flesh; it was made of spirit. Then I saw
shapes below me. When I say "below" I don't mean that
they were physically below me. This is the hardest part
to explain. I was not traveling through physical space.
I was in another world. It was like being on a raft in a
river and watching the landscape go by me. I could see the
"land," the physical world, but I wasn't part of it. I
was in another dimension.

Allen describes his experiences in his etheric body in the
following segment from his Egyptian remembrance:

I felt that I was flying. It was dark at first. Then there
was light. I saw the earth below me. I saw shapes
in the distance—buildings in the middle of the desert. My
body came toward them very fast. Then I flew right
through them. The next thing I knew I was in a crowded
bazaar. I watched women and men dressed in robes
walking by me. I saw people buying food and doing
both good and bad things. I could tell all about the
people. I could see inside them; I could see their feelings.
Good people were very clear and shiny; bad people had
a very cloudy vibration. I saw two men who I knew were
thieves. They looked cloudy and dismal. I saw a woman
being escorted by her husband. I knew she was a very
good person; she glowed.

The Silver Thread

One of the most remarkable past life phenomena is the
silver thread that a person sees extending from his body to
the body of his former self, or to the body of someone with
whom he was very close in a previous lifetime. This phenomenon has come up in fourteen of the cases related to me.

The following two experiences occurred to deLancy

Kapleau, who currently resides with her two children in Toronto. DeLancy left her home in Canada because she felt "drawn back" to the Far East. She traveled with her husband extensively throughout India and Japan. Her visits to these countries seemed to have triggered her past life remembrances and also her subsequent interest in the practice of zen.

I was seventeen and living in Vancouver. I'd closed myself up in my room all day to paint, and I told my mother I didn't want to see anybody; I just wanted to paint. While I was painting, an extraordinary thing happened. I was doing a copy of a picture I had seen of an Indian bazaar, and all of a sudden the whole scene disintegrated and I saw a young girl in the distance. It was a young Indian girl, and she was standing in the very bazaar I was painting. I had come into it sort of like a dolly shot in a film. And she was standing with her hand over a stall to pay for some fruit. I suddenly realized that I had seen this girl before; I'd seen her when I was a child, at a distance, in my bedroom. And I wondered who she was. Eventually the scene disintegrated and disappeared.

Several years later when I was practicing zen in Japan, suddenly I saw the same girl in the distance; she was maybe an inch shorter than I was. This time, however, she moved slowly and steadily forward, without walking. The scene came forward, like cinematography can do, until finally she was standing right beside me in my room. Then I saw that a silver thread ran through my heart into hers. She stood literally inches from my sitting pillow, so that I could see clearly every aspect of her. I saw her long pigtail; I could tell you the exact height of her body, how slender she was; I could even see the dust on her feet from having walked in the dusty streets. She wore a rose-colored sari, had flowers in her hair and a crushed handkerchief in her hands. And I knew, of course, that it was myself, because she was strung on the same thread of consciousness, so to speak. I had a strong feeling that she was not static; there was a strong feeling of movement in her. I had felt that movement myself; I wondered if it was possible to go back, seeing I wasn't just a physical body, and take on this body. I thought it was a much nicer one than I have now. She remained beside me for about fifteen or twenty minutes; then she very slowly disintegrated and went back to her own sphere. I felt that this was myself in my last life, and I even recall my previous name—it was Nandita.

A similar experience occurred to me when I was on a trip to India, in Bombay, in the caves of Alafanta, which are in the harbor of Bombay. It was on my second trip to the caves. On my first trip there I had made friends with the young guide whose studies at the university were very similar to my own. He offered to take me back for a second trip for free. He said, "You'd mentioned to me that you'd like to be alone in the caves. I thought I would take the other visitors around to the back cave. This will give you forty or forty-five minutes alone, if you'd like to do it." I said I'd love to. So off I went.

I was left alone in the cave and I climbed up higher and higher in it, becoming more and more absorbed in the almost echoing silence of the cave. And then I observed a small underground grotto with water which caught glimmers of the light from outside the mountain. And I was sitting in silence for a few minutes, thinking, "What a marvelous place this is!" Suddenly, out of absolutely nowhere, I began to hear the tinkling of bells. There was no explanation for it; there were no people in the cave at all. Just to see, I looked out of the cave, but there was absolutely no one there, no one was even facing the cave. I looked around, and in a few seconds I saw a line of about seven or eight young Brahman boys walking on Puja mats and chanting. Each one was wearing a white dhoti. They all wore their hair twisted into knots on the tops of their heads. They were boys of about fourteen or fifteen, and they were chanting in Sanskrit. And one after another they passed right in front of me, filing out toward the mouth of the cave. They were only about seven or eight feet away from me. I heard them chanting, and as about the third one passed me, I was glancing down at his bare feet when I saw, coming out of my heart, a silver thread. It was attached to this person, and as he passed in front of me a tremendous spasm of love exploded in my heart. Then I watched the rest of them file by. I started after him, and I thought, "I wonder if that was me in a past life." And as they walked out of the cave, they just melted into the sunlight and disappeared.

Standing there I was filled with memories from my previous lifetime in India. I saw clearly that it was not myself in a previous lifetime that I had just seen; it was my husband. I knew that this young man had been my husband in a previous lifetime. In that life my name had been Mukti and his Aditya.

The Guide

In thirty-two cases the person heard a "voice" that guided him through his remembrance. A few people referred to this guiding presence as the voice of their soul. This guide explained to the person why he was seeing specific moments from his former lives and how actions in past lives had affected his development from lifetime to lifetime.

After Pamela Cohen's first past life remembrance, in which she saw herself as a frontier woman in Kentucky, she had a second experience in which she saw short portions of a number of her previous incarnations. During these portions she heard the voice of what she described as a guide.

I first became aware that I was being guided when I heard a voice beginning to talk to me. It was a very strong, sure voice. It wasn't a voice with sound, though; it was a voice that came from inside my mind. The words

were just in my mind, like when you think of something.
I feel it was the voice of my soul.

It wasn't a physical guide; it wasn't in a physical form. It
was just showing me things, presenting them to me.
That is the only way I can describe it. I wasn't controlling
it. I was the audience, and someone was showing me
everything. I was being led through my experiences. The
guide showed me about fifteen or twenty past incarnations
very quickly, one after another. And in every one of them
there was a feeling of desperation and emptiness. Each
lifetime was almost a kind of waste because I hadn't
done what I was supposed to do.

All of them took place in a flash. And I kept thinking,
"Oh, yes, I remember that, and that one too; yes, I
remember that I did all of these things." They were all
painful memories because I could feel all of the misery in
each life, and I was just so bored in each one. You
know, bored with the husband and kids and the whole
bit. But everything the guide showed me I remembered.
All of the thousands of experiences from my past
lives were absolutely true. I recognized them as I saw them
and the guide commented about each one. And I knew
that the guide was my friend and was just trying to
help me.

The Judgment

In some remembrances, after the guide has shown someone parts of his past lives, it begins to comment about the
person's past and current experiences. Individuals who have
experienced the judgment feel that its primary function was
to help them understand why they are faced with particular
obstacles in their present lifetime and to give them an overall
sense of how they are progressing in their cycle of incarnations. People reported that the guide was impartial during
the judgment; it did not condemn them for their misdeeds or
praise them for their successes. They told me that if there
was a feeling of recrimination, it was on their own part.
Having seen that they were failing to overcome their selfish-

ness, hatred, insecurities, jealousies and other limitations, people felt sad that they had wasted so much time in hurting themselves or others. But they reported that the guide was not concerned with whether they had been "good" or "bad" in their past lives except to show them that they were progressing either quickly or slowly. If the guide told them they were doing well and progressing to a higher level in each of their incarnations, it would then encourage them to continue making progress and to transcend their present level of achievement. When the guide pointed out that they were having difficulty making progress in their present life, it would then offer suggestions to help them overcome their difficulties.

Bob works for a large aerospace firm in Seattle. During the Vietnam War he was in the field as a military advisor to the South Vietnamese. One afternoon in May while on a routine patrol he and his squad were pinned down under heavy mortar fire. While waiting for the shelling to stop he had the following remembrance.

I saw several lifetimes. The one thing that was constant
throughout everything I saw was what I can only call
a guide. The guide kept telling me when I had learned
and when I hadn't learned. For example, I saw several
lifetimes in which I was a warrior. There was one in
particular in which I was a Roman officer. I wasn't
a general, but a lieutenant or a minor officer of some kind.
I was a very good fighter and I loved to fight. I had killed
many, many men. One day I was out riding with my
troops. We came upon some Christians, and it was our
job to either destroy them or bring them back with us.
Most of the men wanted to kill them immediately.
But I saw one man I thought I knew from somewhere. I
rode over to him and commanded him to look up at me. I
looked at his face and saw something. I felt that he
was a good man. I told my men that these Christians
weren't worth bloodying our swords on and that we
should press on. We left them there, and the other soldiers

were thunderstruck that I had not ordered the Christians destroyed. I knew I should have, but something I saw in one of the faces had stopped me. We rode on and left them alone.

Now the guide told me that I had done something good. It said that because I had allowed these people to live, I would advance or progress to a higher life in my next incarnation. Then I saw more scenes from that lifetime. I saw myself fighting and pillaging and even raping conquered women. I was a soldier of Rome. What did I care for God and morality? My God was Caesar. But at the end of my life, when I lay dying, I saw all the things that had happened to me in that life pass before my eyes. I saw nothing but the killing and other bad things I had done. I saw one good thing, though, when I had saved those Christians. At this point I heard the guide again. It told me that because of all the harm I had done others I might have suffered in my next life, but because I had done this one positive thing, much of that suffering was not going to take place.

The guide told me that doing one positive thing cancels many of the negative things we have done. It told me that the same was true in the life I am currently leading. It told me to help others instead of hurting them. The guide went on to explain that I could rectify my current mistakes if I would only do positive things that would help others. The guide constantly emphasized that the most important thing I needed to learn in my current life was to love those around me. The guide told me that I should not worry about the harmful things I had already done. If I would resolve from that point on only to do the right things, then I could easily overcome the negative things I had done thus far.

The Chain of Lifetimes

Some individuals reported that the guide showed them an overview of all of their lifetimes. When they viewed this "chain of lifetimes," they were able to see how they had

progressed from one lifetime to another. Some persons reported seeing hundreds of lifetimes, while others saw only
a few.

Most of the people I spoke with about their chain of
lifetimes felt that they had progressed at a very slow rate
from lifetime to lifetime. They felt that God had given them
the opportunity to evolve to a higher state in each life, but
that they had held back their own development by not striving for higher moral and spiritual values.

At the conclusion of Harry's remembrance, he had a vision
of his chain of lifetimes. He said that his particular chain
was very long and that after seeing them he had a sense of
his development from lifetime to lifetime.

> Pearls on a string—that's what they were like. Each
> one was like a little globe. As I looked at it, I got a
> distinct feeling from each one of them. It was like
> looking at photographs from each year of your life.
> You could see how you had grown in each one.

Pamela Cohen also compared the chain to "clear globes."
But her overall feeling after seeing her chain of lifetimes was
that she had "wasted" many of her lifetimes by seeking
physical instead of spiritual fulfillment.

> Clear bubbles, clear globes filled with a kind of
> viscous liquid. Each one was perfect. The guide told me
> about each one, about what each had meant. There
> were many of them. I had the feeling that I hadn't
> accomplished much in them, though. I had lived so
> many ordinary lives and not really done much so far.

Lisa, a social worker in Denver, had a more mixed reaction
to her chain of lifetimes.

> I was amazed by how much progress I had made. The
> first lifetimes I could see didn't seem human. I was

hardly a conscious being. In the middle ones I was
very unkind. I was selfish, vain and egotistical. In the most
recent ones I was no longer like that. I had become
more involved in giving, sharing and loving. I was a better
person.

George is a disc jockey in Memphis, Tennessee. He was
particularly amazed by how long his chain of lifetimes was.

> I couldn't help thinking, "Christ! All of these lives
> were mine! I've been on earth so many times!" There they
> were. They stretched as far as I could see. Each one
> was different. They were hung together like rosary
> beads. That's how I saw them. They made me think of
> the rosary beads my mother always had in church. I saw
> them hanging there in the air. It was like in the movie
> *2001*, where at the end there's a shot of all the planets
> lined up.

The following vision of the "chain of lifetimes" occurred
to Mark, a tool and die maker in Chicago. After the judgment
he felt that he was "flying" above the earth. At this point in
his experience he saw the chain.

> There's no way I can tell you what it was like because
> it was like nothing I had ever seen before. I saw about
> twenty of them. They were stretched in the distance.
> Those that were closest to me were the ones I had been in
> most recently. I knew that those all the way on the
> other side were my first ones.
> I saw them all. This may sound crazy to you, but each
> one told me about itself. Not in words, but in feelings.
> Kind of like knowing without having to think about it.
> I didn't know every little detail that had occurred in
> every one. I didn't need to know that; I wouldn't want to.
> I just had a sense of the important stuff in each one
> of them. It was funny to see that I had been all of those

different people and lived in so many different places. Then they all started to move—that's the only way I can describe it to you. They got bigger and bigger, and I saw inside each one. I kept getting the same feeling. "I've done the same stupid things for so many lives—when will I learn?" When I had had a good look at all of them, they backed off. Then the whole thing just faded in front of me, and then I came back.

THE PROCESS
OF EVOLUTION

*Nature is the evolving phenomenon, while Conscious-
ness is its guide in evolution. At each stage, nature
transcends the limits of its own species and presses forward to new conquests.*

Sri Chinmoy:
Eternity's Breath

The accounts of reincarnation that have been presented to me contain many of the aspects of the reincarnation process as depicted in the *Tibetan Book of the Dead,* the *Bhagavad-Gita,* and other Far Eastern books on the subject of death and reincarnation. Since none of the persons I spoke with was familiar with the reincarnation process before the remembrance, these similarities help to support their contention that their remembrances were indeed genuine. The following theoretical description of the death and rebirth process is intended to provide a brief overview of the reincarnation process so that these similarities will become clearer.

According to Far Eastern doctrines,* the process of rein-

* The philosophy and cosmology of reincarnation presented in this chapter present the major Buddhist and Hindu doctrines on the subject. More detailed information can be gained from the source books listed in the bibliography in the back of this volume.

carnation was started by God when he created the world: There was a time when God alone existed. But He decided that He would gain great joy by creating many worlds, each of which He populated with many different types of beings. God created each of these beings by dividing a portion of Himself into souls, each of which is eternal and passes through a process of evolution in which it gradually grows and develops and finally, after taking many incarnations, attains perfection.

The Soul's Evolution

The Hindus and the Buddhists believe that when the soul is first created it is not fully developed. In order for it to fully develop it must pass through the process of reincarnation. But God does not compel the soul to incarnate. If it wishes, it can stay in one of many beautiful nonphysical worlds. But some souls feel the necessity to consciously evolve toward a higher level of perfection in order to please God. They choose to incarnate into the physical world because only there can they attain complete perfection. Souls who choose to incarnate on earth will eventually reach more advanced levels of development and enjoy much more peace and bliss than those who choose not to.

Souls who incarnate on earth pass through a specific series of stages in their evolution. New souls who are starting their journey incarnate first in the mineral kingdom, then progress through the plant and animal kingdoms, and finally enter the human kingdom. After thousands of human incarnations, in each of which the soul progresses to a higher level of development, it reaches a perfected state and stops incarnating on earth. It will then go to a nonphysical world, where it will continue to exist in a state of total bliss and joy for eternity.

In each of its incarnations on earth the soul incarnates in a body. Normally it will choose to stay in a particular body as long as it can, because it is growing and developing through its experiences on earth. But when it feels that it would make faster progress by leaving its present incarnation and starting fresh in a new incarnation, it leaves the body, and the body dies.

In each lifetime the soul evolves to a higher level. All of the experiences and knowledge it gains in each of its lifetimes is stored within itself. When the soul chooses to leave a particular body, it passes through a number of nonphysical worlds, after which it comes to rest in its own world. After resting, it selects a new incarnation and starts the process over again.

The soul seeks different experiences in each of its bodies. In some bodies, it chooses to experience suffering, poverty, illness and other difficulties. In other incarnations, it chooses to experience fame, fortune and power. But in and through all of these experiences the soul remains in a state of joy. It is only concerned with progressing toward perfection. It welcomes all experiences that will help it to reach its destined goal.

Prehuman Incarnations

The theory of reincarnation stipulates that the soul begin its journey on earth in the mineral kingdom. It will have a number of incarnations on this most rudimentary level before it progresses to the plant kingdom. After many incarnations as a plant, it moves into the animal kingdom, where it will have its final incarnations before passing into its human lifetimes. But at no point in its evolution will it go backward: after having incarnated as a human being, the soul will not incarnate as a plant or animal. In each of its lifetimes, it evolves toward a higher stage of development.

According to the *Bhagavad-Gita*, the principal Hindu text on the subject of reincarnation, the soul was never a mineral, plant or animal. What we refer to as the body is only the soul's outer covering. The soul does not become any of the bodies it takes on, just as we don't become our clothing.

Yesterday a person may have worn one outfit, today another, and tomorrow an entirely different one. But a person remains the same regardless of the clothing he wears. The soul remains the same whether it is "wearing" the body of a mineral, plant, animal or human being.

Six of the persons I interviewed believe they have had remembrances of their prehuman incarnations. In each of the six cases, the person was able to recall one or more of his incarnations in the animal kingdom; none, however, recalled incarnations in either the vegetable or the mineral kingdom.

Wendy lives in Ann Arbor, Michigan, where she is a dental assistant. She had the following remembrance one morning at work. In this section she discusses a previous incarnation in which she was a bird.

I viewed hundreds of my lives on earth. I was this and that person. I went further and further back. I viewed some of my first human lifetimes in which I was little more than a savage. The voice that had been talking to me through all of my visions told me I had been an owl in my last animal life. Then it happened. I became the owl from the inside out, from every possible angle. It was like *flash, flash, flash, flash.* First I would be inside it, then outside it. I saw exactly what I looked like with these orange eyes, and these sort of brown and white feathers. I saw it from every possible 360-degree angle. Then I experienced the consciousness of an owl. It was absolutely blank, like there was nothing in there. It was totally empty. The experience lasted maybe for three minutes. It was absolutely fascinating, like a movie show. At times I was in the movie, and at times I was watching it.

Nat, a computer designer for a small electronics firm in the New York area, had a past life remembrance in which he feels he saw three of his prehuman incarnations.

I had the sensation that I was flying through the air. The ground below me was clear; I could pick out the slightest detail. I was conscious in a very different way. I did not have thoughts exactly; they were more impressions that darted through me. I could feel my bird body pulsing each time I moved my wings. The wind was against me, so I had to pump hard. I felt freedom; I was free to fly and sail in the wind. I caught a breeze and glided; the sensation was unbelievable. . . .

In the next incarnation I was in the water. I felt I was a turtle—a giant sea turtle. I had a sense of timelessness. I can remember being in the water, then crawling on land. I could not see well; the world seemed so bright when I was on land. I remember that the birds bothered me. It seems funny now that I was so incredibly slow on land but so agile when I was in the water.

The earliest one I saw is the most difficult to describe. I was in the water again. I was a whale. I could feel the cold black water moving past me. Eating, hunger, constantly feeding—these were my main concerns. I did not have much awareness, only the feeling of constant movement. I simply ate and swam, although I could feel a kind of protective emotion toward the other whales around me. We traveled in a group, and I was always aware of the others, particularly the young. They needed my protection.

The Human Incarnations

After the soul has completed its cycle of mineral, plant and animal incarnations, it enters into its human lifetimes. The doctrines of reincarnation postulate that although the soul is neither masculine nor feminine, at the time of its first human incarnation it will choose to incarnate in either a male or a female body and will continue in the same sex for all of its future lifetimes.

Souls pass through three distinct stages of development in their human incarnations. Persons who are in their early human incarnations have a limited awareness of their intellect and little or no awareness of their souls. To a large extent they are motivated by their desires for sensory and instinctual experiences, as they were during their animal incarnations. They perceive life primarily through their senses, are ruled by their desires, and have little or no conscious control over their actions. They strive for physical pleasure but find that the gratification received from such pleasure does not last. They may have a limited spiritual awareness in which they see God not as a being of infinite light and love but as a wrathful God who must be propitiated with ritualistic sacrifices and offerings.

The *Bhagavad-Gita* states that after the soul has had many human incarnations in which it allows the individual to be ruled by his senses and passions, it seeks a higher birth. It then prompts the person to develop his mental capacities. During these intermediate incarnations, a person will look at life through his mind. He will discover that intellectual pleasures are more fulfilling than the physical pleasures which he had sought in his earlier lifetimes. Although he derives a greater satisfaction from intellectual than from sensory stimulation in these incarnations, he eventually recognizes that lasting happiness cannot be found in either physical or mental pursuits. After many lifetimes during which an individual is developing his intellectual capacities, his soul will lead him on to the third stage of human evolution.

According to the *Gita*, in the third stage an individual seeks fulfillment through the development of his spiritual self. By entering into states of meditation and contemplation, he discovers that his physical body is only a small portion of what he really is. His continued exploration of the non-physical parts of his being leads him to states of mystical knowledge and spiritual fulfillment. He then consciously progresses toward the higher states of Illumination, Liberation and Self-Realization.

Enlightenment

The doctrines of the rebirth process assert that in the third stage of a person's human incarnations he will enter into a contemplative life. He may follow an established spiritual path such as Christianity, Hinduism or Judaism, or he may formulate a path of his own. But eventually he will seek to attain a higher degree of self-knowledge than he has been able to attain on his own or under the auspices of a conventional religion. At that time he will seek a spiritual guide who has already attained total self-knowledge. By studying with this spiritual master, he will eventually be able to fathom the mysteries of life.

The role of the spiritual master or guru is unfortunately one of the most misunderstood aspects of the reincarnation process. Many people assume that a guru must come from India and that gurus charge large sums of money for their services. In the West in recent years we have seen a flood of self-styled gurus who have managed to make themselves wealthy without leading anyone into higher states of consciousness. People who have had the misfortune to come into contact with one of these false gurus might well suppose that all other gurus are like them. But the fact that we have had one or two bad teachers in school does not mean that all teachers are bad. There are sincere and genuine gurus who, after many years of meditation and contemplation, have attained profound states of spiritual knowledge. They offer their services free of charge to anyone who sincerely wishes to be guided by them. A guru or spiritual master can come from any part of the world. He can come from the Buddhist, Christian, Yogic, Hasidic, or some other school of spiritual development. But, according to the *Bhagavad-Gita*, a true spiritual master is one who has become fully conscious of all levels of reality, who can see and feel God twenty-four hours a day.

Under a spiritual master's guidance, the student makes rapid progress, ascending to higher and higher levels of self-knowledge. The methods employed by various spiritual masters to lead the student to these states of spiritual illumination will vary, but the state of enlightenment they eventually achieve is the same. In most schools of mysticism the most common forms of spiritual practice are meditation, prayer and self-giving. But there is a great deal of variety in how and to what degree these different forms of spiritual practice are applied. For example, in zen the student will usually sit in silent states of meditation (zazen) for many hours a day, while in certain forms of yoga the guru will encourage the student to spend most of his time actively serving the world and helping others.

After a number of years of study in which he has sought to follow the teacher's precepts, the student experiences his first illumination. While he will have a series of progressively higher illuminations on his way toward the attainment of Liberation, his first illumination will have the greatest overall effect on his life. Until that time he may have had a number of glimpses of higher truth. But according to Far Eastern mystical doctrines, when the student has his first illumination he totally transcends the limitations of his physical mind and body and experiences the essence of his soul. He discovers that everything he had thought, heard or read about the nature of existence was totally wrong; these were all conceptual ways of looking at something that could not possibly be understood intellectually. He experiences a bliss beyond expression and in a "flash" perceives the true nature of higher reality.

The experience of illumination can last from a few minutes to a few hours. After the experience ends, the student slowly comes back to a more mundane level of awareness. But his experience has totally changed his understanding of himself and of the world in which he lives. While the immediate effects of his experience will last for only a few days or weeks, it will take him months or years to fully absorb and integrate all that he learned in those few minutes in which he consciously entered into his own soul.

Liberation

After the student has had a number of illuminations, he will eventually attain a state of Liberation from the world of desire. According to Far Eastern teachings, Liberation can only be achieved here on earth; it cannot be attained on any other planet or any other plane. If a being exists in another world or plane and wants to progress to the level of Liberation, he must take human incarnations on this earth and progress through the cycle of reincarnation until Liberation is attained.

Once a being has attained Liberation, he will not fall backward on the spiritual path. Until that time it is possible for a person to be overcome by the forces of desire and illusion and to regress temporarily. But unlike certain learned abilities that do not always carry over from one life to another, spiritual knowledge stays with a soul permanently. If he stops meditating, the essence of the inner knowledge he has achieved is stored within his soul. Either later in his present lifetime or in a future incarnation, he will resume his quest for Liberation. At that time all of his inner knowledge will be returned to him.

When a person has attained Liberation, he can choose to stop incarnating. He has attained a high degree of spiritual knowledge and can stay at his current level of development in one of the nonphysical worlds, or he can choose to return to earth to help other souls reach higher levels of spiritual unfoldment. In that case he consciously returns to the world, but he cannot be bound by it.

The Liberated soul has attained a high degree of spiritual knowledge that is far beyond the level which most human beings have attained. But he has not become totally conscious of Truth and God. If he chooses to become one with God, he must go one step higher on the ladder of consciousness to Self-Realization.

Self-Realization

The Liberated soul is no longer affected by the forces of ignorance. According to the Buddhist teachings, he has worked out his own salvation. Just as there are persons in this world who stop going to school after they have received their college degree, and others who wish to go on for their master's degree or even higher, so in the world of spiritual realization there are some souls who seek to go beyond the state we call Liberation.

A Liberated soul has overcome the desires, fears, worries and limitations to which other human beings are subject. He has attained a state of eternal happiness which he will never lose. But a Self-Realized soul has progressed even further; he has free access to all knowledge and is capable of guiding other souls to Liberation or Self-Realization.

The difference between a Liberated and a Self-Realized soul can perhaps be better understood by the following analogy. A man has a rich friend who owns a big house and will let him come to visit him whenever he likes. The world may be filled with hungry people who live in terrible conditions, but the man is not affected by the conditions of others. Formerly he too lived in poverty and was at the mercy of fate and fortune, but after many years of work he was able to improve his condition and make friends with a rich man. Now whenever he is hungry he goes to his rich friend for as long as he likes. He is no longer affected by the poverty of the world, because his rich friend always provides for him. This is the situation of the Liberated soul. He is no longer affected by the turmoil of life on this earth. He can enter into the Supreme Self at will and stay in the higher nonphysical worlds as long as he likes.

But the Self-Realized soul has gone one step further than the man in our analogy. Instead of only having free access to the Supreme Self, he has become one with the Supreme Self. His rich friend has not only accepted him as a friend; he has made him his equal. He has given him the keys to his house. Everything that was his rich friend's is now his. Instead of visiting his rich friend, he now lives with him constantly.

The Self-Realized soul is a conscious embodiment of the Supreme Self. He has realized his Self. He has become one with his "father" in heaven. The difference between the Realized soul and the ordinary soul is that the Realized soul is conscious of the fact that he is an extension of the Supreme Self that exists within and beyond all of life. He has become a clear and perfect channel for the will and power of the Supreme Self and thus is able to aid others in their spiritual journey. An ordinary soul is also an embodiment of the Supreme Self, but he is not conscious of this fact. Because he is less conscious of his true nature, he is unable to reach his full potential.

According to the Far Eastern perspective, the greatest spiritual teachers of all time—Sri Rama, Sri Krishna, Buddha, Christ, Sri Chaitanya, and Sri Rama Krishna—were all Self-Realized souls. They led their disciples to higher states of existence and inspired the world at large to lead better and higher lives. But, according to these teachings, a time comes when even the Self-Realized teachers no longer choose to incarnate on earth. From that time on, their souls remain in the higher worlds. From these higher worlds they can continue to help persons on earth to evolve by meditating on them and sending them peace, light, bliss and spiritual guidance.

Differences Between Buddhist and Hindu Viewpoints

There is very little overall difference between the Buddhist and Hindu versions of the death and rebirth process we call reincarnation. The primary differences are not so much in the mechanics of the process as they are in the terminologies they use and their viewpoints as to the eventual goal of reincarnation.

The Buddhist path leads to a state of perpetual bliss called nirvana. The souls who choose to enter into nirvana do not return to be reborn. They have finished their play upon this earth.

When one's cosmic play is done, he enters into nirvana. If one is a tired soul and wants to go permanently beyond the conflict, beyond the capacities of the cosmic forces, then nirvana is to be welcomed. Nirvana is the cessation of all earthly activities, the extinction of desires, suffering, bondage, limitation and death. In this state one goes beyond the conception of time and space. This world, earth, is the playground for the dance of the cosmic forces. But when one enters into nirvana, the cosmic forces yield to the ultimate highest Truth, and the Knower, the Known, and the Knowledge or Wisdom are like three angles blended into one. At that time one becomes both the Knower and the Known.

Sri Chinmoy:
The Summits of God Life, Samadhi and Siddhi

According to the Hindu version of the doctrine of death and rebirth, a person can attain salvation through the practice of Yoga. Through prayer, meditation and self-giving, man is eventually able to achieve Liberation and Self-Realization. In this sense the Buddhist and Hindu teachings are identical. But in the Hindu (Yogic) philosophy, an individual is prompted to go beyond nirvana. After attaining Liberation or Self-Realization, he is advised to come back into the world to lead other souls to enlightenment and to try to reveal and manifest God on earth. Those souls who choose to return to the world after they have achieved Self-Realization continue to evolve and reach higher levels, whereas those who choose to enter into nirvana remain at that level of static bliss.

People who subscribe to the philosophy of reincarnation believe that birth and death are doorways through which they walk at the beginning and end of each of their lifetimes, but they do not feel that birth and death marks the beginning or end of their existence. Instead they feel that they have many lives, in each of which they are growing, learning and progressing to a more evolved state of existence. They do not believe in a heaven or hell as such, for they feel that every person on earth will eventually attain perfection and pass beyond the rebirth cycle of this world to higher worlds, where he will exist in a state of perfection throughout eternity.

DEATH, DYING AND OTHER WORLDS

Peace, peace! he is not dead, he doth not sleep—
He hath awakened from the dream of life—
'Tis we, who lost in stormy visions, keep
With phantoms an unprofitable strife . . .
He lives, he wakes—'tis Death is dead, not he . . .

     Percy Bysshe Shelley:
     "Adonais"

Verily, verily, I say unto thee,
Except a man be born again, he cannot see the
Kingdom of God.

     The New Testament:
     John 3:3

The Tibetan Book of the Dead is one of the most ancient texts on the subject of reincarnation. Written thousands of years ago by advanced Yogis who claim to have recalled the passage of their souls between death and rebirth, it carefully outlines both the nature and the types of experiences a soul will have after death. It was kept secret for centuries and was used only to initiate advanced students of Tibetan mysticism into the mysteries of the rebirth process so that their passage through the nonphysical worlds, which the *Book of the Dead* refers to as the Bardo Plane, would be less confusing.

According to the *Book of the Dead*, after death a soul will pass through several distinct nonphysical worlds before returning to earth to be reborn. The soul will spend varying amounts of time in each of these higher worlds, depending on its state of spiritual development. The Tibetans believe that souls that are in either the second or third stages of their human incarnations will tend not to reincarnate so quickly, because these souls no longer desire earthly experiences so intensely as do souls that are in either their prehuman or early human incarnations.

According to the Tibetan doctrines of reincarnation, souls that are in their early incarnations are not so conscious of the process of reincarnation as are more mature souls. These young souls are like children in first or second grade who go to a school but are not yet cognizant of how the school operates. Souls in their intermediate human incarnations are more keenly aware of their passage through the nonphysical worlds; they are like older students who have been in school for a number of years and now have a basic understanding of how the system works and are consciously striving to learn and develop. Souls in the last stage of their human incarnations are like teachers who work in a school. They are no longer subject to all of the rules that govern the students and are consciously aiding other souls in their development.

The *Book of the Dead* explains that immediately following a person's death, he may not realize he has died. After he has recognized that his body has died, he will become distressed and will try—without success—to reenter his old body. After death the soul may linger in its old environment on earth for several days, visiting familiar places where it has lived during its former life. In some cases the soul will also linger to observe its former body's funeral and to see to what extent others mourn its death.

According to the *Book of the Dead*, after the soul has lingered on earth for a time, it will feel a pull to go beyond this world. At that time it will begin its journey through the higher worlds. The first world the soul enters into after it leaves the physical world is a vital world filled with chaos. The *Book of the Dead* describes many unpleasant-looking beings who live in this vital world who try to torment the soul. After staying in the vital world, the soul will then enter into a mental world that is composed of abstract ideas and qualities. After passing through this world, it enters into a number of beautiful psychic worlds filled with pleasing colors, scents, and beautiful beings that will help the soul on its journey. Finally, the *Book of the Dead* describes the soul's own world, where it will rest and reflect upon the experiences it has had in its most recent lifetime. After it has rested for some time in its own world, it will retrace its course and be reborn.

Remembrances of the Higher Worlds

Fifteen persons with whom I have spoken claim to have recalled the passage of their soul through the nonphysical worlds. In these cases a person had a remembrance in which he experienced full participation in one of his past lives. But instead of his remembrance terminating during some point within that lifetime, he believes that he reexperienced his death at the end of that past life, the passage of his soul through the higher worlds after his death, and his rebirth in his next incarnation. In each of these cases of between-life remembrance, people experienced similar phenomena in exactly the same sequence. It is also interesting to note that although none of these persons were familiar with the *Book of the Dead* prior to their remembrance, their descriptions of both the order and nature of their experiences are strikingly similar to the descriptions of the death and rebirth process found in the *Tibetan Book of the Dead*.

Samuel is the manager of a large department store in Chicago. He lives with his wife and five children in a large three-story home on the south side of town. In July of 1975 he took his wife and children on a camping trip to Canada. Early one morning while watching the sun rise over the mountains, he had a remembrance of one of his past lives, his death in that lifetime, and his soul's passage through the higher worlds. The majority of the features we have just examined in between-life remembrances are joined together in this section of Samuel's highly detailed remembrance.

I remembered a past life of mine in, what I would guess, judging from the style of dress and the cars, was around the 1930s. In that life I owned a small business in a small midwestern town.

I was walking quickly along the sidewalk when I felt a stabbing pain in my chest. My whole body reeled and I felt incredibly dizzy. I tried to steady myself, but I was seized by a wave of nausea. I reached out to try to support myself and found myself falling toward the ground.

The pain got much worse. I closed my eyes and felt myself gasping for breath. My heart was pounding so loudly that I couldn't even think. I opened my eyes for a moment and saw that a crowd of faces were gathered above me. A man I had seen working in my building was reaching down and loosening my necktie. One woman was telling someone to go get an ambulance. It was then that I realized that I had had a heart attack.

Another wave of pain shot through me, much worse than the first. Everything around me grew hazy; then I felt my whole body spasm and shudder. A series of pictures from my childhood appeared before me. They were followed by scenes from my youth and then scenes from my adult life. I saw the most important stages of my life passing before my eyes in seconds. Then I was swallowed up by blackness and lost consciousness.

I have no idea how long I was unconscious. I was in unfamiliar surroundings in a room somewhere. Everything appeared to be very misty and hazy. I could see some people in the room, furniture, curtains. I could even hear them talking. But they seemed like phantoms to me; they didn't seem solid. I walked over to them and asked them who they were and where I was. They ignored me. I repeated my request. They seemed very agitated by something; the woman was crying, and those around her were trying to comfort her. I became very impatient because they were ignoring me, and I moved closer to them. It was then that I began to suspect that something was wrong with me. I noticed that I didn't exactly walk over to them but sort of glided next to them without having to physically move. I peered at the woman who was crying and at those around her. They seemed very familiar to me. I felt that I had known them at some earlier time in my life. With shock I recognized that the "woman" was my wife. She was surrounded by my two sons and several of my relatives. I called them by name and asked them what was wrong. Still they didn't seem to hear me. I was in a quandary as to what to do. Then I remembered going to work that morning and having a heart attack. A funny thought entered into me. "I'm dead," I thought. "Well, now what am I supposed to do?" Then I was filled with a feeling of self-pity. I thought, "Oh God, I don't want to be dead. Everyone I love is here and they can't even see me." I felt miserable and watched them helplessly.

For a time I watched the people in the room. They were putting on their coats and hats. Their movements seemed very mechanical, as if they were robots or humanoids. I felt alienated from them. I felt the urge to go with them. An outside force was compelling me, pulling me to go. I found myself outside my house beside my car. I saw my brother-in-law driving it. This made me mad. I started to tell him not to drive my car when I realized again that I was dead. It really didn't matter whether he drove it or not.

Then I felt myself moving forward again. I saw that I could move anywhere I wanted to at will. I just wished where I wanted to be, and I was there almost at once. I wished to go with my family, and the next thing I knew I was in a room crowded with people. I found I didn't have to work my way around the crowd but could actually walk through the people there.

Everyone's attention was directed to the front of the room. I saw with some surprise that my body was lying there in a coffin. I was seized with an immediate feeling that I wanted to get back into my body and be alive again.

But at the same instant I also knew that this was impossible; my body was dead, and it would never be alive again. All I could do was wait and watch. I saw all of the people I had known come and see me. I saw my family, friends, even the priest from my church. I was very interested to see how upset many of them were. I could see that some people were very disturbed and cried a great deal. Others had just come because it was expected of them. This angered me. I saw the expression of each one. Then I felt the force moving me again. I had seen enough; I wanted to leave.

I cannot tell you how long I stayed on earth because I had no real conception of time. I wandered from place to place, visiting all the familiar places I had been during my life. I went to my mother's old house, my old high school and many other places. Finally I sensed that I had to leave the earth. I didn't belong there anymore. . . .

I found myself in another world. There were terrible sounds all around me. I could hear a constant thundering and whistling, also loud booms and unhuman cries. The place I was in was filled with broken things, twisted wreckage like a scrap heap. The air was filled with hazy smoke. There were lots of different beings all around me. Many of them were fighting each other. Their howls and cries were so loud that I wanted to run away. I roamed in this world for a long, long time. Occasionally I would see other people like myself. I felt like a stranger in a strange land. Several times the beings there—awful-looking things that were like deformed people—tried to bother me. I found that if I ignored them, they would go away.

Then I left that world and found myself in a realm of ideas. This was a nicer world than the other one. It was filled with voices, singing, music, things like that. I was different in this world myself. That is, when I was in the twisted world my body had been similar to the one I had used on earth after my death. But that body had left me when I came into this world. Now I was not physical; I wasn't shaped like I had been, with hands and arms. I was lighter and clearer. It was more like I was an essence. . . . I stayed in this world and then passed to an even more beautiful one filled with many different-colored lights. They were beautiful. I could hear a kind of music all the time. But it wasn't music in the way that we normally think of music. All of existence was in a kind of harmony. Life itself was music. My being was different in this world too—it was lighter and more luminous. I liked it here very much. It was in this world that I saw people I knew who had died before me. My father and several others I had known came. They greeted me. They did not look like they had on earth. They were luminous beings. But I knew who they were. They welcomed me with great joy.

Then I passed into an even "higher" world. It had millions of levels. I could see levels below me, but not really above me. The light there was dazzling. I could see that the beings on the levels below me were not as aware as I was. I rested here; I knew it was a place of rest. I was infused with a golden light.

The rest seems so remote now. When I saw all this it was clearer, but even then I couldn't have described it. There aren't any words for it. It is being with God; that's the best way I can describe it.

The Experience of Dying

Persons who had remembrances of their physical death in one of their previous lives stated that immediately following the onset of death they saw a review of events from their earliest childhood to the day of their death. Watching the scenes before their death, they were able to gain new insights into the mysterious workings of the death and rebirth process. A Baptist minister recalls:

I saw thousands of pictures flow before me. I saw my mother when I was very young; I saw myself taking

my first steps; the time I fell off my bicycle; when I stole
something from a 5-and-10-cent store; making love with
my first girlfriend; graduating from high school; getting
married; our honeymoon; having children; my wife's
illness; the death of friends; my own aging; everything.
Watching, I learned about myself and what I had seen and
done. I saw my whole life in a minute or two.

Following the review, there was a loud "buzzing" or "ringing sound." After hearing this sound, they had a sense that
they were no longer in their physical bodies. Several people
described seeing their former body "below" or "near" them
and remember wanting very badly to reenter it. Others
recall being confused and not realizing for some time that
they had "died."

Harry remembers:

I saw my body just lying there on the bed. My eyes
were closed tight and I could see I wasn't breathing. I
wanted to be back in my body. I felt terrible. I didn't
know what the heck was going on. Then I knew I had
died and that I could never go back to that body again.

Most people recalled being aware they had died almost
immediately after their "death." But in three cases they did
not accept the fact of their death for what seemed a much
longer period of time. In these cases the person had died in
a violent accident, which caused them to be disoriented.
They roamed the earth for what appeared to be some time
before accepting the fact that they had died.

An elementary school teacher from Bangor, Maine, had a
remembrance in which he saw his death in a former life,
which occurred when he was climbing a mountain. In the
following section of his remembrance he recalls his death and
some of the events immediately following it:

I was English in that life. I was on a mountain-climbing
expedition. One of the men in front of me lost his grip
on a rock and fell back on me. I tried to hold on but

lost my grip and plunged straight down. I remember finding myself alone farther down the mountain and wondering what had happened to the others. I saw a body lying face down in the snow and assumed it was the other fellow who had fallen on me. I walked away from his body and moved around the lower section of the mountain. I wanted to find the others, but I was unsure of how to go about it. I looked for them for a long time before I finally returned to the site of what I believed was the other man's body. Then it dawned on me: I was dead. This wasn't his body—it was mine.

People reported that during their remembrance, after the person they had been had died, they discovered they had a new body that could move through solid objects and travel to places thousands of miles away if they simply wished themselves there. They visited the places in which they had lived before and roamed the earth in that body until they felt a pull to go to another world.

Some individuals recalled lingering beside their former bodies after they had died so that they could observe how others reacted to their death. They derived some satisfaction from watching the grief of their friends and relatives. Two people recalled being angered by the fact that the people they had been close to in that former lifetime grieved for them so little.

Five people reported that at the time of their death in a previous life they saw coming to greet them friends and relatives whom they had known in that lifetime and who had died before them. In these instances the individuals felt that seeing these persons helped them make the transition from life to death. Two others described "luminous beings" who came to guide them on their way to the other worlds. But all of them reported that they eventually felt a growing necessity to move on beyond the earth. They then recall passing through a succession of higher worlds before being reborn into their next incarnation.

William is an electrical engineering student at the State University of New York. He had a remembrance in which he saw a former lifetime in Italy. In the following account he recalls his death in that life and then seeing two of his relatives who had died before him coming to greet him:

I was in the market doing some shopping. It was while I was looking at the vegetables that I began to feel dizzy and sick. I fell to the ground, and my body started to convulse. I felt hot pains stabbing my chest. I heard some of the market women scream, and then I was not part of my body any longer. I was seeing all the action from across the street on the other side of the market. I watched them carry me away, but I didn't much care; it seemed to be happening to someone else. Then my mother and my little brother came to me. Both of them had died before me. They came and took me and led me into another place, a different kind of realm. They looked just like they did when I was living, only younger. My mother—I don't remember when she looked so beautiful. And my little brother was smiling and happy because I was going to be with him.

The Higher Worlds

From the descriptions of people who have had conscious remembrances of their passage through the nonphysical worlds, it would appear that each of these worlds is strikingly different. In each case people described four separate worlds through which they passed after death. The first of these worlds, which I have termed the "vital world," is a dark, murky place inhabited by unhappy and tormented souls. The second is a "mental world" filled with ideas, pleasing shapes, and artistic qualities and essences. The third world is a "psychic world" filled with beautiful light. This is a world of tremendous joy in which many "luminous beings" exist. The fourth world is the "soul's world." People felt that their soul rested in this world and prepared itself for its next birth. While some persons have reported seeing additional worlds, or subsections of these worlds, all of them have reported passing through these four worlds.

The Vital World

People describe the vital world as a place of tremendous chaos, restlessness, dissatisfaction and incompleteness through which, apparently, the soul must pass after death and immediately preceding rebirth. One person described it as looking as though "a cyclone had hit it." Another indicated that it was filled with "many broken and deformed things"— ugly beings who are constantly fighting with one another. Others describe the vital world as a very dark and frightening place that is hazy and filled with smoke. In the following account Allen recalls an experience he had in the vital world after the end of his Egyptian incarnation.

> I felt like I was in a foreign country. I had a body but it was not physical, although it was the same shape as my physical body had been. I found myself in this bleak landscape, and near me there were two people fighting and arguing. The fight was one of tremendous violence; one of them had the other by the neck and was trying to throttle him. Both of them had disheveled hair, and they were shrieking like beasts. And although they kept hurting each other, it seemed as if they could not do any permanent damage to each other. The shrieks coming from them were so ungodly, so appalling, that my only thought was to get away from them. They fought on and on without getting tired. . . . I thought I recognized someone I knew, a friend who had died several months before me. I was happy to see him at first. I stepped out in front of him and called his name. He said something to me that was very rude and pushed me aside and went right past me. I was very unhappy in this world.

When the time came for me to leave, I felt like I was being let out of prison. It was a great relief to leave that place behind.

No one who has had a remembrance of his experience in the vital world has liked being there. But some people seemed to adjust better than others to their stay there.

Several individuals felt there was a correlation between the way they had acted during a past life and the experiences they had had in the vital world after that life. People who felt they had lived a good and selfless life on earth did not seem to suffer so much in the vital world and were not bothered by the beings that lived there. Individuals who reported that they had led a selfish life in which they sought only their own fulfillment were very unhappy in the vital world and were tormented by the beings they encountered.

Harry describes the experiences he had in the vital world after a remembrance of one of his lifetimes.

I was killed in an accident. I saw myself dying, and then I saw myself going into the other worlds. . . . The first world I came to was a terrible place. You have to understand, though, that when I saw this world I wasn't watching it from a distance or anything like that; I was experiencing it myself. It was dark, like a polluted city. Everything there was dirty and ugly, and it was filled with terrible creatures. I saw them bothering other people who were there. They were chasing them and trying to scare them. They didn't come after me; they left me alone. I wondered why this was, and I sensed it was because I had been a missionary. I had spent all my time helping others and giving of myself. I believe that because I was so good I was protected while I was there. I sensed that those "things" bothered people who had been bad in life. People suffer there who have done wrong things in life, but those who have been good don't suffer so much. This place wasn't hell; it was a kind

of purgatory. It was just a place that you pass through
on your way to better worlds.

Theodore is a Russian translator who works for the Department of Defense in Washington, D.C. In the following
segment of his remembrance he describes his experience in
the vital world:

> I found myself in a disgusting place. I was tormented
> by the people there. They were deformed and awful.
> They kept chasing me and asking me questions about my
> life. It was a nightmare. One of them, the biggest one,
> kept asking me why I had harmed people during my life
> and if I enjoyed it. I knew the life I had led had not been
> good. These "things" that kept bothering me seemed to
> know that also. They kept tormenting me. I cannot tell
> you how long I stayed there. . . . There was no feeling
> of time passing.

During their passage through the vital world, people report
that they heard many unpleasant and frightening sounds.
Most commonly reported were (1) a constant thundering
sound; (2) a sound that crackled like fire; (3) sounds of
howling winds and crashing waves; and (4) sounds of earthquakes and avalanches. In addition to these four primary
sounds, many persons reported hearing a variety of shrieks
and cries and the tinkling of bells. They expressed the feeling
that these sounds were in some way connected with the
powerful forces that they felt were operating in the vital
world.

Persons I have spoken with about their passages beyond
death were not able to explain clearly how they moved from
one world to another. As nearly as I can interpret the phenomenon, they felt a "pressure" which pulled them along,
and as soon as they surrendered to it, they found themselves
in another world. Their passage between the worlds was in-
stantaneous.

The Mental World

The mental world was described as a place in which all knowledge exists in "seed" form. During people's stay in the mental realm, they were capable of contemplating hundreds of ideas and concepts at a time. Instead of having to go through an analytical thought process to find an answer to a question, they knew the answer even before the question had formed in their mind. Several people said they witnessed the movement of knowledge from the mental realm to the earth. They described "carrier beings" who transported knowledge to people on earth who were trying to discover or invent something. They also stated that knowledge from this world usually reaches the mind of a person on earth without that person's being conscious of its place of origin. The person on earth assumes that he created the idea himself, not realizing that he has unconsciously borrowed it from the mental world.

People who have had remembrances of the mental world have said that a person who devotes his life to intellectual and artistic pursuits on earth spends more time in this world. This was the case for John, a classical musician who lives in Madison, Wisconsin. In the earlier portion of his remembrance he saw two of his most recent lifetimes. In these lives he had been actively involved as a writer, composer, and musician. After seeing these lives he then recalled his experiences after death.

It was a great place. I would have been happy to have stayed there forever. I could create a complex of ideas in an instant. I was in a state of rapt contemplation and simply enjoyed pure knowledge in all its pristine clarity. I was in a world filled with ideas, symbols, images, and higher conceptions. Millions of them were swirling all around me. It was never confusing; they were all so clear to me. Whenever I wanted to know something, it would appear at once. I did not have a body there. I was pure thought. My thoughts were not couched

in words; they were energy. All of my thoughts had
different colors, and I understood their essence by
seeing the colors. It was a world of abstract existence.

When a person leaves the mental realm, he leaves behind
him his "mental body." In each of the worlds he passes
through after death, he leaves a part of himself behind that
he no longer seems to need. Persons describe this process as
"automatic" or as "happening by itself." After leaving the
physical body in the physical world, the subtle body in the
vital world, and the mental body in the mental world, all
that remains is what most persons describe as their "soul" or
"life principle." In the descriptions of the remaining worlds, I
will use the word *soul* to indicate that essential portion of a
human being which remains with them from lifetime to lifetime.

The Psychic World

Persons I interviewed about their passages through the
different worlds have indicated that each succeeding world
was "brighter" and "higher" than the previous world they
had passed through. Each was less like the physical world,
and they seemed to find it progressively more difficult to
express clearly their experiences in these higher worlds.
Their reasoning was that the experiences they had in the
psychic and soul's world have no counterparts on earth. Most
persons found it easiest to describe their experiences in these
worlds through analogies and comparisons.

During her remembrance in San Diego, Joan witnessed her
death in a previous lifetime. She then recalled her experiences between death and rebirth. In the following section of
her remembrance she reflects on her experience in the psychic
world.

I felt that all my life I had been dressed in a costume
but I didn't know it. One day the costume fell away
and I saw what I really had been all along. I was not what

I thought I was. All my life I had thought of myself as a person, as a body. I thought to myself, "I am so and so, a woman, a mother, a secretary," and things like that. When I went into this world I realized that all along I was not those things. I was a soul, not a body. I couldn't die; I couldn't be born. I lived forever. I wasn't a male or a female. It was like waking up after having amnesia. I was overjoyed to be "me" again. I had been all along, but I had lost sight of it and thought that I was a physical body. My body was only a thing I used for my life on earth. When it wore out, I got rid of it.

It would appear that the psychic world is a very beautiful realm filled with light, peace, joy, and harmony. Many persons report that there is a constant music in the psychic world unlike any music they had ever heard on earth. They describe it as being filled with "the message of life." As they listened to it, they understood themselves and the nature of reality. The psychic world was also described as being filled with "pleasing scents and fragrances of flowers," "beautiful lights," and many "luminous beings of all types." Upon their arrival in the psychic world, people were filled with ecstasy and "complete bliss."

In the same remembrance in which he saw his Egyptian past life, Allen reported that he encountered "beautiful beings like angels" during his passage through the psychic world.

There was nothing but joy there, and colors—such beautiful colors. These were not like the colors on earth; they were deeper and richer. They had sounds and scents too. . . . There were many types of beings there. Beautiful beings like angels. They came to me and helped me. They were so innocent and pure. They told me that I would soon be going to an even higher world where I would rest and that they were here to help me understand everything that was happening to me.

Harry also came into contact with these beings in the psychic world.

> I never believed in angels and all that sort of thing.
> I must admit I was wrong. Not that they have wings and
> halos—that's not it. They are lit up; they are so bright
> it's dazzling. I don't think they were the highest beings,
> the most advanced, but they were helpers. They were not
> in bodies like ours. They were so light and clear that
> it was difficult for me to perceive them at first. Some of
> them were sort of superficial, like a bunch of giggling
> fourteen-year-old girls. They were all very sweet and
> innocent.

Many people have reported that when they entered the psychic world they were greeted by friends and relatives who had died some years before. They did not have physical bodies as they had on earth, but people knew them intuitively. They recognized them by sensing them. One man remembers:

> I saw my wife, the soul that had been my wife. We had
> been together for many lives before. She greeted me. I
> felt such love for her, and I felt her love for me. She
> was a globe of light. There were other globes there too, but
> I knew her right away from the others. She wasn't
> a "she" like she had been on earth when I knew her. She
> didn't have a sex; neither did I.

After a time, people stated, they left the psychic world and progressed to what they called the soul's own world.

The Soul's World

From the descriptions given to me by individuals who have seen it, the soul's world would appear to be composed of countless levels and subworlds. These levels seem to be in an ascending order that is based not on physical height but on the amount of "light" that is present. The lower levels are darker (although most persons report that this so-called darkness is much brighter than sunlight) and the higher levels are brighter. According to those who have had remembrances of this world, souls come to rest in the level that corresponds to their own stage of development. The "new" souls who have not had many lifetimes on earth and are relatively undeveloped come to rest on the lower levels. Those who have had many incarnations and are highly developed ascend to the higher strata and rest there. The souls in the lower levels do not appear to be aware of those above them and cannot visit them. But the more advanced souls from the higher levels are aware of those on the lower levels and can visit them and help them if they choose to do so.

Joan remembers:

I found myself in a vast place. I felt as though I had
come home. I had no apprehensions, fears or worries.
I no longer remembered my former life on earth. Nothing
existed for me but a quiet fulfillment. I was not conscious
of time in the usual sense; everything seemed timeless.
I felt as if I had always been there. It was similar to
the feeling I have when I wake from a dream that has
seemed very real, only to discover that it wasn't real but
only a dream. That is how I felt. My former life on earth
had been a passing dream which I had now awakened
from.

I did not have the sense that I was moving in space.
Everything was consciousness and pure awareness;
there were no dimensions there. I moved through
thousands of levels. On each level different souls were
resting before being born again. The lower levels were
much darker. I somehow knew that the souls on these
levels were not as mature as those on the higher levels.
Finally I reached a level that I was comfortable on. I

stayed there. I sensed that there were many levels above the one I had stopped at and that souls that were more advanced than I would go there.

People describe their experiences in the soul's world as a time of resting and "assimilation." They have said that during their stay they reviewed all of the experiences they had in their previous lifetime. They then assimilated this information and stored it within themselves for future reference.

Artistic Worlds

The descriptions of the soul's world usually include a description of several different worlds within the soul's world. Several of these subworlds are realms of pure art in an unmanifested form. People reported that each art form that man has evolved on earth has a counterpart in one of the artistic worlds. There is a world of higher music, a world of dance, a world of painting, a world of poetry, and many others. When a soul wants to create in these worlds, his creation occurs instantaneously. On earth it may take an artist weeks and months to get a creative inspiration. Then it may take him even longer to execute his inspiration and create a work of art. As soon as a soul projects an idea, that idea becomes a reality. In these worlds a composer can write a symphony in an instant, a painter can see his pictures form instantaneously, and a writer can write a book within seconds.

According to persons who remember experiences in these artistic worlds, all of the art that exists in these worlds exists in an uncreated form. It is the individual's soul which channels these artistic ideas and brings them into being. His own experience of creating art is a kind of art itself.

Alice is an art teacher and sculptor who lives in a small town in southern Indiana. In the following passage she reflects on the nature of the art worlds and recounts her experience there.

There is a constant activity in these worlds of art,
but it is a joyous activity. It does not have any of the
vulgarity of activity in the physical world. In these worlds
it is all a play of light. One experiences sound as a
form of light, and if music is played, there is a correspond-
ing display of light related to the tonalities that are
sounded. The same is true of perfumes and flowers
and so forth. And since there isn't the heaviness and
obstructiveness of the physical mind to contend with,
intention is brought to fruition very quickly, and creative
people, of course, have a time of tremendous joy.
Painters can paint anything in the time it takes to snap
your fingers. Composers can compose just like that. They
create endlessly here, with a freedom they could never
find when they were on earth. And their creations are
so much more beautiful. Instead of having the usual
number of colors in the physical spectrum, an artist has
many more colors that exist in these worlds but not on
earth. The same is true of musical tones, and so on. I visited
several of these worlds and observed many souls
creating there. I also had the feeling that there were many
more of these art worlds that I did not see.

Rebirth

The Buddhists believe that the soul of an average person
will normally take from six to ten years to reincarnate. They
stipulate, however, that in the case of very new souls, mature
souls, or souls that have just left a very difficult lifetime, this
time period can vary. The Buddhists believe that new souls
reincarnate often. They normally take a shorter time between
death and rebirth because they desire worldly experiences.
However, souls that have had thousands of incarnations and
the souls of advanced spiritual masters can spend forty,
fifty, or even hundreds of years between their lifetimes. The
Buddhists also feel that if an individual has had a particularly
hard life in which he has had to fight against constant oppo-

sition, his soul may be especially "tired" and will require more time to rest between lifetimes.

The Far Eastern doctrines of the rebirth process assert that after the soul has rested for a number of years in the soul's world, it will choose a new incarnation and descend into the physical world. The soul will select its next incarnation according to the experiences it feels it needs for its current level of growth and development. This theory will become clearer if we imagine that the soul is like a student who has just been graduated from high school and is trying to decide which college to attend. The student is limited by his grades. If he has high grades he can get into many colleges, but if his marks are poor, he will not have so many schools to choose from. In much the same way the soul is limited in its choice of possible incarnations by its level of development. If the soul is highly evolved, then, like the student with good marks, it can choose among a greater variety of possibilities. But if the soul is not very advanced— like the student with poor marks—it will not have so wide a selection. This theory also postulates that occasionally an advanced soul will choose to incarnate with a family in which the souls are not so developed as it is, or that an undeveloped soul will sometimes incarnate with a family whose souls are more advanced. But as a rule the soul will choose a family along its own lines of evolution. If the soul were to choose a family in which all the others were far more advanced, it would be in the predicament of a student who chose to go to a school where the other students are much more advanced than he. Occasionally a soul will select such a birth in order to be elevated by its association with more advanced souls. An advanced soul will incarnate with a family of souls that are not so developed as it is if it wants to help those souls to advance or if it simply wants the experience of incarnating with such souls.

The next step in the rebirth process, according to Hindu philosophy, occurs when the soul has an "interview" with God. God then either approves or disapproves of the soul's choice. If He disapproves, the soul has the option of choosing another location and family, or it can continue with its original choice. God will not force a particular choice upon the soul. Once the soul has settled on a choice, it passes through a number of worlds and finally comes to rest in the foetus (in the human incarnation) of an unborn child. According to the Hindu theory, the soul usually enters the foetus in the last few months of pregnancy, but in some cases it can choose to incarnate at the moment of birth, or even several minutes after birth. Then, settled in its new life, it continues its long passage to Liberation and Self-Realization.

In the following section of her account, Joan describes her experiences before her rebirth in her current lifetime:

I felt I was waking from a long dream. I had been resting for so long. I felt it was time to go forward, to return to the field of life. I was aware that I had a lot of things to accomplish in my next life. I could not fail as I had before. It was very important that I strive to be more conscious of everything, once I was reborn. It was easy here being without a body. It was all clear. I knew when I returned to the world a temporary amnesia would overcome me. I would forget my purpose and my mission; I had done this each time. This time I sensed that I would remember sooner. I resolved then and there to become fully conscious in that lifetime, to overcome my imperfections, to strive for something higher, deeper, and purer than my usual round of experiences. I had lived many times. I had known love, hate, fear, death, disease, hardship and plenitude. But through all of these experiences in all of my lifetimes on earth, I had not found lasting joy and satisfaction. I was well aware of the fact that I was making progress in each lifetime; I was happier, I had overcome more of my imperfections, but that was not enough. I wanted to be on earth as I was here, totally conscious of my existence. To realize that I was not simply a person, but that I was part of God,

an extension of Him. This I would forget on earth. But I
was determined to strive for that higher awareness.

In this segment of Harry's remembrance he reflects upon
his rebirth into his present life in America.

I knew I wanted to live in America. I wanted to be
reborn into a family I had been with before. I knew the
souls in that family. I had been with them for many
lifetimes. I wished to rejoin them. I did not have to tell
this to the Supreme Being; He knew. I felt He approved.
I started my return to the world of humans.

Myron is a clerk in a camera store in a small town in
Delaware. In his past life remembrance he saw his death in
a previous life that he had led in Germany. He then recalled
his passage between his death in his German life and his
rebirth into a Chinese family. In this section of his remembrance he reflects upon his vision of God that occurred
shortly before rebirth.

I saw God. He was beautiful beyond description. No
words, no pictures, no language could ever describe Him.
All forms emanated from Him; I saw all of the universes,
all of the persons, all of the worlds contained in Him.
I expressed my feelings to Him, my sorrows at having
failed before. He seemed undisturbed by my failures. He
was encouraging me to try again. With this new inspiration
I came back to life, determined this time to help others,
to serve the world, and to become fully conscious of
both my inner and my outer existence.

KARMA—THE LAW OF CAUSE AND EFFECT

Be not deceived; God is not mocked: for whatsoever
a man soweth, that shall he also reap.
For he that soweth to his flesh shall of the flesh
reap corruption; but he that soweth to the Spirit
shall of the Spirit reap life everlasting.

The New Testament
Galatians 6:7–8

Karma is a Sanskrit word meaning action. The law of karma is found in the Hindu and Buddhist teachings of the process of reincarnation. The essence of the law also appears within the framework of the Judeo-Christian religions.

Simply put, the law of karma says that every time an individual acts, whether his action is on the physical, mental, or psychic level, he creates an effect that will be returned to him either in his current lifetime or in a future lifetime. Once he has absorbed the effect of his previous action, he is freed from that action; he does not have to experience the results of his good or bad actions indefinitely. The law further states that every person, object, and nonphysical form is bound by karma until it achieves liberation from karma. Until someone is liberated from his past, present and future karma, he must continue to be reborn on earth.

The Hindu and Buddhist theories of the operation of the law of karma are basically the same. According to these theories, the karma a person amasses in each of his lifetimes determines the circumstances under which he will be born, the major incidents and occurrences that will happen during his lifetime, and the opportunities and obstacles that will help or hinder him as he walks down the pathway of life. There is an overall karma that binds all things, but when an individual soul enters its first human incarnation, a direct karma begins to be amassed.

In an individual's first human incarnation he will perform both good and bad actions. The law of karma states that for every positive action he performs, a positive action will be returned to him; and for every negative action he performs, a negative action will be returned to him. But the results of these actions will not necessarily return to an individual in one lifetime. The karmic results of both good and bad actions are usually received over a number of lifetimes.

It will be easier to understand how the law of karma works if we can imagine that when an individual enters his first human incarnation he is given two karmic "bank accounts." All of his positive actions from that lifetime are recorded in one account and all of his negative ones are recorded in the other. Each time he performs an action, he receives a deposit in one of his accounts depending on the nature of his action. These karmic "deposits" will be returned to him in the forms of opportunities or obstacles that he will encounter in his present and future lifetimes. Each human being on earth is constantly creating new karma, and unless he is in his first human incarnation, he is also experiencing the results of his actions from his previous lives.

Freedom from activity is never achieved by abstaining from action. Nobody can become perfect by merely ceasing to act. In fact, nobody can ever rest from his activity even for a second. All are mercilessly forced to act.

—*Bhagavad-Gita*

The law of karma explains that many of the so-called injustices of our world are not really unjust but only appear to be so because we do not see that karmic justice is at work. If, for example, we observe a person who is always harming others and doing wrong things and who seems to be succeeding in spite of his wrong actions, it would indicate that in a previous lifetime he performed good actions and is now reaping the reward for those good actions. But in the future, in this lifetime or in a distant lifetime, he must pay the penalty for the bad karma he is now creating. If, on the other hand, we see a person who performs only good actions, who is always giving of himself and seeking no reward for his actions, but who constantly experiences problems and difficulties in his life in spite of the fact that he is being good, we must understand that although this person is being good in this lifetime, he has committed some wrong actions in a past lifetime and is now paying the penalty. Once he has worked through his bad karma and learns not to make the same mistakes again, he will not have to reexperience his bad karma. If from that point forward he will create only good karma, in the future he will experience only the positive results of his actions.

According to the law of karma, karma is not only created by a person's physical actions but also by his mental and psychic activities. The Buddhists and Hindus believe that if someone is constantly projecting negative or harmful thoughts, others will project negative thoughts toward him. This is the karmic result of his thoughts. If a person hates, he will in turn be hated. But if he has positive thoughts and emotions, positive thoughts and emotions will be returned to him. If he loves, love will be returned to him. The karma that an individual reaps on the mental plane need not be returned to him in his present lifetime. Although he may sincerely love others in this life, he may be greeted with hate. But in a future lifetime the love that has been given to other people will be returned to him.

Mental karma does not have to be returned by another individual. It can also be directly returned to the person who created it in his own mental and emotional state of mind. If an individual projects hates, doubts, and jealousies, his mental karma can return to him in the forms of frustration, despair and depression. But if someone projects love, peace, and joy then his mental karma can be returned to him in the forms of happiness, inspiration and clarity of mind.

Neither the Hindus nor the Buddhists believe in the conception of sin. Instead they believe that God exists in all things, both the good and the bad. From the Christian point of view, sin is a result of evil. Christians believe that evil is an absolute force that will always remain such. In the Judeo-Christian tradition, when a person commits a sin he is punished. If his sin remains unabsolved by God, he will be punished eternally. But the Hindus and Buddhists believe that there is no such thing as evil; there is only Light and less Light. Since God exists in all things, they reason that all things must therefore be good.

According to this view, God exists in different degrees in all things. He exists in both the light of wisdom and the darkness of ignorance. The purpose of karma is to teach a person to prefer the light of wisdom to the darkness of ignorance, to lead him to perfection by showing him where he has left the path that leads to truth and to encourage him to return to that path.

Another way of looking at the contrasting Eastern and Western points of view is to imagine that there are two different schools in the same town. In one school, children are encouraged to be good. If they are good they are given a reward. But if they fail to be good, they are severely punished or thrown out of school. In the other school they also encourage the children to be good. But when the children fail to be good, they don't punish them; instead they give them special lessons that will teach them to do the right thing. When they do something positive they are encouraged; they are given a kind of reward. If they give someone a present, they will get a present in return. When they hurt someone, they are hurt in return. The hurt that is inflicted on them is not a punishment; it is a means of showing them what the hurt feels like. Knowing this, they will not hurt anyone again. In this school the children are never thrown out; they keep coming to classes until they become perfect.

Karmic Remembrances

A large percentage of the people who have had remembrances expressed the idea that their actions in past lives affected their succeeding lives. They observed that when they did positive things in a past lifetime, they later reaped the reward for these actions; and when they performed harmful actions, they later had to pay the penalty. The following two remembrances were given to me by persons who saw how their actions in a past lifetime adversely affected them in their current lifetime.

Mario works for a phone-answering service and lives in Jersey City, New Jersey. He was involved in a terrible accident in which he lost his sight. He subsequently had a remembrance in which he saw that his blindness occurred because of his actions in a prior life.

Four years ago I was blinded in an industrial accident in
the plant where I worked. Ever since then I have
cursed God and my fate for blinding me. I have always
tried to be a good person, and when I lost my sight, I lost
all faith in the justice of God. One morning when I was
sitting alone I had an experience; I was given my sight
back for a few minutes. But instead of being able to
see what was in the room around me, I was able to see
back into the past.
I was taken back into another time. I saw a king.
He ruled a great country on the other side of the world.
He was a very good king, and he was very fond of his
wife's niece. His wife, the queen, was extremely jealous
of the king's affection for her niece, and she plotted to have
her niece killed. On a certain night an assassin was to
come to kill the girl when she was sleeping. But the king

found out about the plot and saved the girl. He had
his wife brought before him, and in a fit of rage he had
her eyes put out. I saw that I was that king in a previous
time, and that I lost my sight in this lifetime because I
blinded my wife in a past lifetime. I no longer blame God
or curse my fate, because I know that I deserved to lose
my sight in this life. It is easier for me to live now.

Leon lives in Chicago. He teaches karate and judo and in
his spare time coaches a boys' soccer team. He and his wife
are unable to have children, and although they have visited
many different doctors, they have never been able to find a
satisfactory explanation. But in a vision of one of his past
lives Leon discovered what he believes to have been the
cause of their problem.

We have never been able to have children. My wife
and I never adopted a child because we believed that
one day things might change. We visited many doctors
and clinics, but none of them have been able to tell us
why we can't have children. In desperation I went to
a church to pray to God to find out why. During my prayer
I had a vision. I saw myself in a jungle. I was walking
with a large group of other men. We were all carrying
spears. We came to a village. There were only women
in the village and old men; the young must have been
away. We attacked the village and killed everyone there. I
killed one of the women who was pregnant. As she was
dying, she cursed me. It was revealed to me that because
I took her life and the life of her unborn child, I will
not be allowed to have children in this lifetime.

Many persons I interviewed believe they also have been
able to trace the chain of positive events that led to their
good fortune in their current lifetime. Nelly works in a
stationery store in southern Connecticut. She recently won
a large sum of money in a state lottery. She has had visions

of several of her past lives, and not long after winning the lottery she had the following remembrance:

I saw in a past life that I was born into a well-to-do family in England. After my parents died, I inherited a large sum of money. I gave much of my inheritance to charity and used the rest to set up an orphanage for poor abandoned children. I ran the orphanage for many years until one winter I caught the fever and died. It was because of my giving of myself and my money in a past life that I have been so fortunate this time.

An airplane pilot from Philadelphia recalls:

My life has been very easy. There's some kind of protecting force looking out for me. Many times I have been in life or death situations, but I always seem to make it through. During the Second World War I was shot down over enemy territory. It was a miracle that I survived the crash-landing. My plane was destroyed, but I didn't break one bone.

I was befriended by many people and eventually smuggled back to England. This thing happened to me when I was crossing the mountains making my escape. We came to a pass in the mountains and paused to rest. I was sitting with my guide from the underground who was leading me out. I figure I wasn't used to the altitude, and I must have lost consciousness. The next thing I knew, I was in a town. The people were dressed like Arabs. The buildings were made out of a whitish sandstone. It was midday. People were walking, doing their marketing and trading. I felt I was standing in a courtyard, but I never tried to move or look at myself—at my body, I mean.

At the end of the market opposite me was an old man. He was dressed in robes that were old and worn. A group of young boys were seated at his feet; he seemed to be

instructing them in something. I kept looking at his
face and having the feeling that I knew him from
somewhere. I wanted to go over and talk to him, but I
didn't seem able to move from where I was. All at once
I felt myself moving forward and going toward the man.
It was so fast—I was standing next to him, and the next
moment I was him.

I was looking at the boys at my feet; I was seeing
them from the old man's point of view. I had been a
wealthy landowner. I had spent every waking moment
of my life in earning more and more money. One day I
met a man who told me of a higher truth. I listened to him
speak, and his words touched my heart. He told me to
renounce my belongings and live humbly and simply. I
was so moved by what he said that I started to live a
spiritual life. I gave my possessions to others and spent
my time teaching and giving instruction. I saw that my
later years had all been for the service of others.

When I was seeing these things, I heard a voice talking
to me. The voice was explaining that good things came
to me in this life because I had been kind to others in my
past. The voice told me, "You will return to your country
after the war. You will live and go on to work for others.
You must love others. You must serve others. This is
where true happiness lies. Those who have wealth, fame
and pleasure only delude themselves. These things only
rob them of their real treasures, their awareness of truth.
In this life you do not need to give all your belongings
away as you did then. You need material things to help
you help others. What is important is not your wealth
but how you use it. If you help others with it, then it
is good. If you use it selfishly, then you gain nothing
and will be unhappy."

The voice said other things about how to run my life.
It assured me that I would live, which seemed unlikely to
me at the time. I did live, and I have tried my best to
follow the advice of the voice. It is true what it said

about being happy. I am happiest when I help others.
I use a great deal of my free time in community service
projects and in helping members of my family.

One of the questions people frequently ask regarding the
law of karma is: What determines which actions are considered to be good karma, and what actions are bad karma?
As we know, in one culture certain activities are accepted as
natural, whereas in another they would be viewed as ab-
normal. For example, in one country it may be considered
immoral to work on a Sunday, but in another country Sunday
is treated like any other working day. Therefore, would it be
bad or good karma to work on a Sunday? According to the
Buddhist view, it is not the culture that determines what is
good or bad karma; it is the nature of the action and the
intent of the person who performs that action. Any action
that harms another individual becomes bad karma. But just
as our own legal system recognizes the importance of a
person's intentions when committing a crime, so too the law
of karma appears to make similar allowances.

If a person commits a premeditated murder, his punishment in our legal system is much more severe than if he
killed someone in a quarrel or in self-defense. Even though
in all three of these cases one person has killed another, a
judge would render three different verdicts and prescribe
three different sentences. In the same way the law of karma
takes into consideration not only the person's intentions,
but also his stage of development. If a child commits a crime
we do not punish him so severely as we do an adult who
more fully understands the consequences of his action. In
the same sense, the law of karma will not apply the same
justice to each individual who commits a particular offense.
The more aware a person is of wrongdoing, the greater the
karmic penalty will be. The chain of actions and reactions
that extends from lifetime to lifetime applies not only to
actions that help or hurt others but also to actions that a
person performs that help or hurt himself.

Those who recalled committing suicide in their past lives have said that the penalty for their self-destruction was incalculable. They had to go through a long period of time before they could reincarnate, much longer than persons who have died of natural causes. They further stated that they actually regressed after their suicide, and they then had to go through many other lifetimes in order to attain the level of development they had reached before they had taken their own lives. These extra lifetimes were usually quite horrible. In most of them, the suicides were born physically crippled. Those who were not appeared to be prone to mental illness. Often they had a very negative effect on the family into which they were born, creating all kinds of problems and disturbances in their relatives' lives. Only after many of these painful lifetimes did they work out what they describe as their penalty and start to lead normal lives again.

It would appear that in some cases of suicide, extenuating circumstances can lessen or totally wipe out this karmic penalty. When a person commits suicide to escape an ignoble death (as in the case of a soldier who has been captured by the enemy and kills himself rather than allowing the enemy to destroy him), there appears to be no penalty. For one who is dying of natural causes in a particularly painful or degrading manner (as in the case of a terminal cancer patient who commits suicide instead of watching his body slowly deteriorate), there appears to be no penalty. In instances in which a person sacrifices his own life so that others may live, or when a husband or wife dies and the other partner prefers death to living without his mate, there appears to be no penalty. The punishment is apparently applied to the person who has committed suicide to escape from problems and difficulties that he could have overcome had he tried.

The following statements were made by persons who have recalled their suicides in previous lifetimes.

Willie is a taxi driver in Detroit. In the following segment, he reflects on his remembrance of his suicide in a past life and its repercussions:

I was sure it was wrong to do it. The entire time I was dying I kept thinking, "My God, what have I done to myself?" When I left my body I knew that I wasn't going where everyone else went. I went into an awful world. The pain was worse than being boiled alive in oil. My lives, when I started to be born again, were terrible too. I was born deformed, mongoloid; I died as a child. It was terrible. I had to accept it; it was my fault. I had thrown away the gift of life. After many, many of these lives I feel I was forgiven. I had learned my lesson. Then my lives were like before. It all came back to normal again.

Jack is a student at the University of Texas. While sitting in a chemistry class he had a spontaneous remembrance in which he saw what he feels was his most recent past lifetime.

I was a prisoner of war. They used to beat us every day. We had no food, and the men around me were dying like flies. I was forced to do hard labor and then beaten. We found out that our troops were coming back. They were going to kill us all before our troops could rescue us. I killed myself by swallowing broken glass. . . . After I died, an angelic being came to me. She told me that I did not have to suffer for killing myself because I wasn't running away. She told me that those people who made me suffer would suffer in the future.

Elaine works as a waitress in a resort hotel in Miami, Florida. She had a remembrance of a past life which she feels took place in India.

I saw one life in which I lived in India. My husband died. In India at that time it was the custom for the wife to die with her husband, to go into his funeral pyre. I wanted my soul to go with my husband's soul. My life was meaningless without him. I gladly threw myself into the fire. I died with great love for him.

I did not suffer because I had ended my own life. I made a strong bond with my husband's soul because of what I

did. I was with him in many lives after that because I had
so much love for him. God was aware of why I did it and
forgave me. He allowed me to be with him again after
that because my love was so strong.

According to Far Eastern doctrines, although the law of
karma is binding for all people, it is possible, through the
grace of God, for a person to skip over much of his bad
karma. If God observes that an individual is truly sorry he
has done wrong and will not repeat his mistake, He can
nullify that person's bad karma. Since the purpose of karmic
retribution is not to make the individual suffer but to teach
him, if he has already learned his lesson it would be point-
less for him to be subjected to the same experience again.
His situation in this instance is analogous to that of an
individual who has committed a crime, has been caught and
sent to jail, but is released early because he mended his ways
and will no longer commit wrong actions.

Within the past few years the word karma has become a
part of our own language. Often in a conversation we hear
someone refer to something bad that happened to him as
his "karma." When he refers to karma in this way, he is in
effect saying that what occurred to him (his karma) was
fated and that there was no possible way of avoiding it. But
this attitude is not a clear representation of the Far Eastern
theory of karma. According to the Hindu and Buddhist texts,
one should never linger over or worry about one's past karma.
This only binds him more firmly to his karma. The Hindus
feel that even the worst karma can be negated when a person
sincerely tries to lead a higher and better life. All karma can
be nullified when an individual sincerely aspires only to
Higher Truth.

Myra is a physical therapist. She grew up in the North-
east and moved to the Pacific Northwest shortly after she
finished her professional training. In the following section of
her remembrance she describes why she feels that God
nullified some of her bad karma:

The lifetime I saw was terrible. I was a prostitute in
Italy. I would sleep with men and then steal their money.
I saw a time when I even killed one of them when he
caught me taking his money. I stabbed him to death.
I felt that I was going to suffer for what I did. My life
changed, though. I got the sense that because I help
others so much in this life, because I am always doing a
lot of free clinic work and because I really care about my
patients, those bad things I did are not going to affect me
now or in the future.

According to the theory of karma, there is a second instance in which karma can be nullified. When a person is
guided by a Self-Realized guru, the guru can, if he chooses,
accept some of the burden of his student's bad karma. The
guru has the capacity to transfer the student's karma to himself and work the karma out for him so that the student can
make faster progress. Gurus do not do this with all of their
students, because in many cases the student needs to experience his karma in order to learn. But the guru will accept
the burden of his student's karma if he sees that by re-
lieving him of a portion of it, the student will be able to
attain Illumination sooner. When the guru takes the student's
karma upon himself, he is acting as a strong person who is
helping someone weaker than himself. This may be better
understood by the following analogy.

The guru is a guide who leads the student to Truth. Truth,
in our analogy, is on top of a high mountain. The guru can
climb up and down the mountain at will; he knows the way
and can easily lead the student. But if someone has to carry
a heavy pack while he is trying to follow the guru up to the
mountaintop, he will make very slow progress. If the guru
can take the student's karmic "pack" on his own back and
carry it, the student will be able to discover Truth sooner.

Justin is a Franciscan monk. One evening during vespers
he had a vision of a past life which he believes took place in
Tibet.

Well, the main thing I remember was living in a monastery there. Everyone dressed in ochre-colored robes. My parents took me to the monastery in that life when I was only twelve. I studied with the master of the monastery. He seemed to take a shine to me right away. I was his personal attendant, bringing him food, washing his clothes, doing things of that nature. I venerated him because I knew he was a very holy man. I was ill, though; there was something wrong with my heart. I became sick very easily and wasn't as strong as the other monks in the temple were. The master changed all of that for me. He explained that my illness was the result of the bad things I had done in past lives. He healed me by taking it upon himself. Then my heart was fine; I did not get sick the way I had before. I lived to serve him for many, many years.

TWIN SOULS, SOUL MATES AND KARMIC CONNECTIONS

When to the sessions of sweet silent thought
I summon up remembrance of things past,
I sigh the lack of many a thing I sought,
And with old woes new wail my dear time's waste;

Then can I drown an eye, unused to flow,
For precious friends hid in death's dateless night,
And weep afresh love's long-since-cancelled woe,
And moan the expense of many a vanished sight. . . .

But if the while I think on thee, dear friend,
All losses are restored, and sorrows end.

William Shakespeare:
"Sonnet 30"

We have many different types of relationships throughout our lives, but there are usually a few people to whom we feel especially attached. At times we have intense relationships with people for reasons that are not clear to us. We may discover that we have become very close to a person with whom we have little in common, yet there is something that draws us to that person. We will make great sacrifices and travel thousands of miles simply to be near him or her.

There are other individuals toward whom we feel an immediate dislike or animosity. While these persons may have done nothing to hurt us, we feel very uncomfortable in their presence and breathe a sigh of relief when we can avoid them.

Many of the people who had past life remembrances felt that the source of these unaccountable emotions between two people was a prior relationship in another lifetime. During their remembrances sixty-three people recognized a person in their present life as someone with whom they had been associated in a previous life. I have divided these multiple-life associations into three categories: twin souls, soul mates and karmic connections.

According to the Far Eastern theory of reincarnation, twin souls are persons with similar talents who incarnate together for several lifetimes. Soul mates are persons who are totally compatible. They usually incarnate together for many lifetimes. Karmic connections are persons who are joined together by experiences they share. They are not necessarily compatible and will incarnate together for fewer lifetimes.

Twin Soul Remembrances

From the nineteen twin soul remembrances presented to me, it would appear that twin souls are persons who have similar interests, capacities, and attitudes. They share experiences in several of their lifetimes. For example, two friends who are both musicians may decide to work together in a certain lifetime. Since they are alike in many ways and gain a great deal of joy by sharing their experiences, they will incarnate together for a number of lifetimes so that they can continue to enjoy their relationship.

The following four remembrances depict the relationship between twin souls. The first occurred to Lewis, a securities analyst in Chattanooga, Tennessee.

I studied economics at the University of Tennessee in Knoxville. When I was in my junior year there I had a good buddy who I spent most of my free time with. We would do everything together—we would play basketball, go out on double dates, study together. We were so inseparable that people used to tease us about it. Both of us wanted to become economics majors. Both of us liked to study the market, and eventually we both wanted to work for securities investment houses. We never paid much mind

to it, though; it seemed natural that if you had a good
buddy who was interested in all the same stuff you were,
you would hang together as much as possible.

I was in my senior year at U.T. and was spending a
weekend studying in the fraternity house. There was a
football game away, and the campus had pretty near
cleared out. My buddy and I had to study for a big exam,
and we were more into basketball anyhow. We were
studying in the same room when I had a vision. I saw us
together in another life. We looked different, but I know
for sure it was us. We were in England. We were both
lawyers. The time was—I would guess—around the end of
the nineteenth century. I saw all kinds of different
moments from that life. And let me tell you it was just
the same then as it is now. We did everything together.
We studied at the university together, went drinking
together, everything.

Mary Ann is a young mother who lives in California. Her
husband drives a truck for a national moving company. She
grew up in Los Angeles. When she was in high school she
made friends with Laurie.

I had one girlfriend, Laurie, who was always so much
closer than the rest of my friends. We went to high school
together in Los Angeles. After school we would go to my
house or hers and talk about boys, school—those types of
things. We had the same likes and dislikes. I remember one
time we each went shopping to get dresses for a dance.
I picked out the one I liked the best when I went shopping
with my mom and she did the same. That night we got
together to see each other's dresses, and do you know we
got the exact same ones!

We went through all the same stages: boys, getting
married, having children. It got so we practically didn't
have to talk at all. I could tell what she was thinking all the
time, and vice versa. I could even tell if it was her calling
me on the phone. I would say, "Hello, Laurie," when I

picked up the phone if I felt it was her. I was right almost all the time.

Laurie developed cancer about a year ago. She must have had it for some time. She was so thin and everything. They gave her chemotherapy and cobalt treatments, but she only got sicker and sicker. We both knew she was dying. I went to her room one night in the hospital, when she was near the end. She was in so much pain that even the most powerful drugs didn't help at that point. She would go in and out of consciousness; it must have been the drugs. I was alone with her, sitting by her bed, holding her hand, when suddenly the room changed and I wasn't there anymore. I felt like I was going down a long tunnel. Then I came out of it, and I was outside in a big field. I was watching lots of children playing. There were two ladies watching over them. I felt I knew them from somewhere, but I couldn't exactly place it. Then it came to me. It was Laurie and me in another life. We had been sisters before. These were our children we were watching. All kinds of memories came back to me. There were seven children in the family that we grew up in, but Laurie and I were the closest. We were alike then like we had been all of our lives this time.

This is the strangest part. All the time I was looking at this, I was aware of Laurie. I had been holding her hand and I could still feel it, kind of like in a dream. It seemed far away. When I was seeing us together in the past, I felt her hand squeeze mine. I could tell she was seeing this too, at the exact same moment. After it ended I could tell too. Before, she had been very agitated, but she was very quiet after. I did not feel so bad when I saw we had been with each other in the past. I think that because we are so much alike we came together again in this life, and I believe that we will be with each other in our next life.

Laurie died a week later. I was heartbroken. But seeing the past and believing that we may be with each other in the future helped me accept it better. I wanted to tell the other members of Laurie's family about my experience, but I was afraid they would not understand or would think I was overcome with grief.

A retired executive in Florida had the following remembrance concerning a childhood friend:

Many times I think about my friend Ralphie. We sure enjoyed each other's company. Our parents lived in the same village. Ralphie and I would play in the woods all day when our parents were not making us help them around the house. We grew up and went into business together. We were partners for over twelve years until we sold the business and I went into advertising. I went to work for B.B.D.&O. and Ralphie went to California to open another business.

Ralphie and I had shared a common interest in war. Ever since we were kids we would play war, read books about it and discuss battles. We even enlisted together and fought in Germany. We were in the same company. But long before all of that happened, when we were kids, I had a remarkable experience.

One day Ralphie and I were playing soldiers. I forget exactly who was the enemy and who was the good guy. I was running through the woods looking for him when I discovered I was changed. I was not a kid but a young man. I was a soldier. I was out walking near the place where our army had set up camp when I heard a voice calling me. I turned and there was my friend. It was Ralphie. It wasn't the same face and he was grown up, but I recognized him instantly. He was a soldier with me, and he was coming to find out what I was up to. I'll never forget the way he flashed his teeth when he smiled. It was so nice. The vision only lasted for a minute at most. It ended, and there I was back in the woods alone.

The following twin soul remembrance occurred to the curator of a museum in Boston. He told me that he had been close friends with two of his co-workers in the museum for

some time and that whenever the three of them were together they felt that they were in some way related to one
another, although in this life they had had no previous
connection.

I was sitting with two very dear friends of mine. Both
of these girls are very close to each other and close to me
too. When the three of us are together we feel something
very special. We were sitting together in my house one
night when something unusual happened. I closed my eyes
and I was transported into another time. I saw three
Indians. One Indian was clearly a chief. He had a beautiful
body and was wearing a headdress full of feathers. I saw
him standing on top of a boulder and looking up into the
sky. He was very muscular, and his skin seemed to glow
with health and virility.

Behind him were two Indian girls who I think must have
been his wives. They were both quiet and reserved. They
just kept looking at him. Suddenly I was looking at the
whole scene from a different angle. I could see that above
the chief, very high up in the air, an eagle was slowly
flying in great loops over his head. I felt that I was in the
sky above the eagle. I recalled then that I had been that
chief, and my two friends had been my wives in another
lifetime.

After my experience I found myself back sitting with my
friends. The incident had taken place in a flash. I related
what I had just witnessed, and then I told my friends how
ever since I was a child I had been drawn to American
Indian artifacts. They said that they had also always been
interested in American Indian culture, and the two of them
agreed that my vision stirred similar memories within
them.

Soul Mates

In twenty-eight remembrances, a person saw that he had
been associated in several of his past lives with someone in

his current life. When the two had first met, they felt magnetically drawn to each other, often without knowing why. They found that they were happy to be together regardless of their activities. Eventually one or both of them had a remembrance in which he saw that they had had a similar relationship in many of their previous lifetimes.

It would appear that one can have more than one soul mate, and that soul mates can be of either the same or the opposite sex. In the following remembrance, a well-known film star describes his encounters with two of his soul mates:

In this life I have met two of my soul mates. I met the first one in the summer of 1977. I was making an appearance in a university town in the South. I lecture frequently at universities and colleges. I enjoy the contact with young people. I don't really need the money anymore, but it gives me a chance to communicate with people.

That night there was a large crowd. I was scheduled to give the main lecture, and the next day I was going to hold several smaller seminars. It was a warm and muggy night. I came out and started to warm up the audience by telling them a couple of funny stories. They were a good crowd and responded well.

I have a habit of looking at one or two people in the audience when I give a lecture. I focus my attention on them when I speak and I watch their reactions. I can get a pretty good idea of how well I'm doing by observing them. This particular night I scanned the audience and automatically settled on one of the girls sitting close to the front. I watched her throughout the show. I'm so familiar with the talks I give that I can detach myself from them. I can set myself on automatic pilot and think of other things. Well, the thing I kept thinking of was the fact that I wanted to see this girl after the show. I was drawn to her. I actually couldn't wait until the show ended so that I could go and speak with her.

Everyone there enjoyed my talk. After the applause

quieted down, I looked to see where she was. I lost track of
her in the crowd, and I was so busy signing autographs
and answering the usual battery of questions that I
couldn't get away to look for her. I like to spend as much
time talking to people as I can, but it was late and they
had to close the room. We started to leave, and my host
asked me if I wanted to go out to eat. I was engaged in a
conversation with several of the students, so I said, "Hell,
yes; let's bring them with us." We took the students along
and went to a local restaurant.

Standing by the door of the auditorium was the girl,
with two of her girlfriends. I said hello to her as I passed
and then I stopped. I told her if she and her friends wanted
to join us they were welcome to. They agreed, and I had
my host give them directions to the place.

At the restaurant I talked with all the students. But
the girl I was interested in was sitting at the far end of
the table, so I didn't really get to talk with her. She and her
friends stayed with us for a while and then left. I wanted
to speak with her, but I felt foolish and didn't know what
to say. When she walked behind me as she left, I felt
something like an electric current between us. I had no
way of knowing that she was the one who was passing
behind me, yet I knew. I stayed up half the night talking
as usual, and finally they dropped me off at the Holiday
Inn at around 2 A.M.

The next morning they sent a car for me. I got to the
university for the seminars a few minutes late. I hoped that
the girl I was so drawn to the night before would be there.
I walked in the room and looked over the students, but
she wasn't among them. I decided the best thing to do was
to put the whole thing out of my mind. I took a break
after the seminar and did an interview with a woman
reporter from the local paper. After that I came back for
my second seminar. I looked around the class, and to my
surprise she had arrived.

All through the seminar I found myself looking at her.

I supposed I was just attracted to her because she was good-looking. She was short, had a thick angular face, and wore a light-colored summer dress. I am aware of how I am with women, and so I decided not to speak with her. I thought that if there was something special between us, she would feel it too. I waited to find out what would happen.

When the seminar was over, she walked up to me. She had brought some papers she wanted me to look at. Standing in front of her, I wanted to reach out and touch her. I felt so close to her, I was happy just standing with her. The two of us talked about the papers she had brought, but both of us were aware that the conversation we were having had nothing to do with what we were really feeling. I took her to the cafeteria and had a Coke with her. She put her hand in mine, and I could feel the funniest sensation. Walking down the hall, I felt first like I was inside my body, then inside hers. My perspective would change back and forth. With our hands clasped, it felt like we were one person. We talked, and then I had to return to give the last seminar. She sat through it and we kept looking at each other. I had to leave immediately for a plane after the seminar was over. She asked me if I wanted to stay for another day and spend time with her. I told her that I couldn't because I was expected in New York for another engagement. I invited her to come to the airport with me.

We rode in the car listening to my host talk about nothing. I wasn't aware of anything but her. I didn't even listen to him, and that's when I felt the past. Riding in the car I remembered her. She had awakened memories in me from another life. Little pictures formed inside my mind. Then we arrived at the airport.

We exchanged phone numbers and I told her to call me. We embraced. You must understand that this girl was a complete stranger to me. I had been with her for only a few hours. This is not the kind of thing I normally do.

I talked with her once or twice after that. We were very drawn to each other, but I could tell she was a little afraid of me. While I was there it was all clear to her, but with the distance between us she started to doubt her experience. I haven't tried to contact her because she has to realize the connection by herself. I never told her the part about the past lives because I didn't want to confuse her. I have regretted the fact that I didn't cancel my other engagement and stay with her. I don't think I have ever felt so much from another human being in such a short time. Sometimes I can feel her; I get her vibrations. Even though I don't know where she is or what she is doing, I am aware of her presence. I think someday she will be drawn back to me. I don't think she was ready to handle the experience at the time. I feel she must come to me. I can only wait and see.

The second experience was much clearer to me. This could be because I was prepared by the first experience I had with the girl in the South. That experience was very strong, but I really didn't see much of what my past life with the girl had been. It was more of a certainty in my mind, a voice telling me, "You've been with her for many lifetimes."

This time was on a Sunday night. I was memorizing some lines at my home. The phone rang and I answered. A friend of mine wanted to come over and visit, and she had some people with her. I told her to come over, and I went back to work. An hour or so later there was a knock on the door.

There were four of them. My friend Sally, two other girls and another man. We sat in my living room and had a drink. I felt very happy. I ignored one of the girls whom Sally had brought and spent my time talking with Sally, the other girl and the other guy. I was more aware of the other girl, but I didn't know what to say to her. I felt that the two of us were having a private conversation even though the others and I were talking verbally. I felt the same kind of closeness for this girl that I had felt for the girl in the South. Something told me I had been with her in many lives before, but I didn't see any pictures of it; I just knew it.

They were going to leave when I told her to call me. It was out of the blue and surprised her. Before she went out the door I sent her upstairs to see my room. I don't understand why I did this; I simply heard myself telling her to do it. She went upstairs by herself, looked around, then came down and left with the others.

A day or two later she called me. I told her that I would like to see her and that I would be in the city on Saturday and she could meet me there if she wanted to. We made arrangements and hung up.

That Saturday we got our signals crossed. I had been anticipating meeting her and I was very excited. I got held up at the studio and didn't get to the restaurant where I was going to meet her and the people who had been with her that night at my place. I felt depressed about the whole thing. This isn't like me. Women come in and out of my life and I'm unattached to them. I love them, but I never feel I have the right to hold on to them. I'm happy when they are here and I'm happy when they are gone. It makes it better for everyone that way, especially me. But this girl was different. I felt sad that I had missed her, and I had only met her once. I went home, resolved not to call her. I assumed that it was like the girl I had met in the South: I was aware of the connection but she wasn't. She probably thought I was after her body.

That night the phone rang, and it was her. She apologized for leaving the restaurant and explained that her friends had wanted to go and she had given in to them. We made arrangements to have her come to my house alone the next day, and then we hung up.

We didn't get together the next day until around eleven P.M. When she arrived at my house, we were both pretty tired. We sat and talked for some time, and she told me that she felt drawn to me. The interesting thing about our mutual attraction was that it was not at all physical. We were very happy to be together. She told me that she felt that she was "complete" when I was with her. She said it was like finding a part of herself that had been missing all of her life. I felt exactly the same way.

We stayed up talking all night. Somewhere between three and four in the morning I had a vision of our past lives. I say I had a vision, but actually we both had a vision. Afterward we described to each other what we had seen, and it was exactly the same. We were both able to see the same past lives at the same time.

I remember that the vision started with my feeling light-headed. I felt that I was rising out of my body and flying. I let go of my body and found myself in another land. I saw hundreds of scenes, one after another, from our past lives. We had been with each other in many lives—in Egypt, in Europe, in South America, and in many other places. In each lifetime I could see that our relationship was developing and becoming even closer. In some of our earlier lifetimes we were friends. In our Egyptian incarnation we were lovers. In our European incarnation we were more artistically inclined and shared our love of the arts. In our South American incarnation we were very involved in religion. We had even died with each other in one of our lives. One thing remained the same constantly throughout our lifetimes; it was this total love for each other. We loved each other so much that we would find each other in almost every life.

As I was telling you, we discussed what we had seen, and it was the same. This proved to me that it wasn't my imagination or anything like that. We have since become the best of friends, and we spend as much time as possible with each other. I am so happy that I have found my friend again. We understand each other in every way. And we kind of balance each other out. If I need to feel happy, I simply have to be with her and I am at peace.

We don't think about our past lives. Our relationship now is new. I don't think the past matters anymore.

In the following remembrance Tony, a young artist who lives in San Francisco, relates an experience he had with a soul mate, John, who lives in New England. In this account both soul mates are of the same sex.

I first met my friend John at a meeting with my guru. I had been studying meditation for four years. My guru lives in the East, and I go there every August for several weeks of intensive meditation with him. John lives in New England. The only time I get to see him is every year in August. I first noticed him at one of the August meditations. At the end of meditation the guru always gives food to everyone who comes. John was in line and I found that I was watching him. I liked him immediately and felt drawn to him. I felt an inner connection with him, you might say.

I got to know him better the next year when he came out to California on a trip. He stayed at my house for a couple of days. I was busy working at this restaurant just off Market Street. I arranged to get a day off so the two of us could take a trip to see the redwoods over at Muir Woods.

He picked me up in a car he had rented. It was a beautiful clear, windy day in the spring. We drove across the bridge and headed up into the hills.

We arrived at the redwood forest and walked around the trails for about an hour. We stopped at the site that is dedicated to Woodrow Wilson and meditated. Then we walked on up some of the higher trails.

It was very quiet in the woods. Except for the sounds of one or two birds, all we could hear was the sound of our own feet walking through the undergrowth. We were both very inspired by the feeling of eternality that we had standing underneath the giant redwoods. Neither one of us said a word.

When we were walking down the trails, I flashed on some moments from our other lives together. They were quick and complete glimpses of moments we had shared hundreds of years before. The first one I saw was the two of us walking down a path like the one we were on. We were both American Indians. We were brothers in that lifetime. Then I saw the two of us in China. We were traveling down a river in a small oriental fishing boat. We were escaping from a prison camp of some kind. We had broken the unfair law of the Emperor and we had been sentenced to death. We had escaped at night by surprising one of the guards and knocking him out. We managed to find some people headed downriver who took us on board. I had the feeling that we made a successful escape, but I didn't see that part.

We continued to walk through the redwood trails. Some light dripped down on us, filtering itself in patterns from the trees overhead. I felt that we were walking through a giant cathedral. Each step I took brought me back to someplace else we had been before. The important thing was that in each of the lives I saw we helped each other spiritually. I have had many so-called friendships both now and in my past in which people hurt me and I hurt them. My relationship with John was always positive. Whenever I am with him I get a tremendous joy. I live in San Francisco and he lives 3,000 miles away, but this doesn't seem to affect our closeness. I know the changes he is going through. When I am thinking about calling him, he will call me first. If I write him a letter, he knows what I have written about before he opens it. I have a feeling that in this life we are going to work together in a most important way in the future, although our occupations are different. There is a stillness, a very deep, quiet and refined stillness, when we are together. We know each other within that stillness.

In a letter she sent me in April of 1978, deLancy Kapleau described two past life remembrances she had when she was a child. Her subsequent meeting with a soul mate she believes she saw in one of these remembrances convinced her of the validity of her past life visions.

This took place in Winnipeg, before I was two. I was standing in my crib, supporting myself on my arms and staring at my window curtains, which were gently flapping in the breeze. It was midafternoon. I had awakened from my nap and was waiting for my mother to come and dress me. Like a fog disintegrating, the room began to fade away. My attention became progressively pinpointed around this singular revelation. I now perceived myself to be a person of great antiquity. I laughed with consternation. "What on earth have I done? I've come back again! I'm a baby all over again! Totally dependent on elders! And for years this will go on!" I knew with the same unequivocal certainty that I was standing on my own two feet, that I had lived as a human dozens and dozens of times before. Seemingly interminable lives stretched away into the past. The curious thing about this incident is that interwoven in some way through it was the vague feeling of failure, as though I were here because I had not succeeded in things in my previous lifetimes. Then, in the middle of my reveries, I found myself once more a baby.

The second occurrence was in Calgary, when I was five. My mother was in my room, putting me and my younger sister to bed. I lay silently watching her picking up our toys, putting away our clothing, and mildly scolding us for our untidiness. I always felt great security from my mother. Her love was strong and radiant, and her capabilities more than enough to protect us from anything and everything. Quite suddenly the walls began to fade, and I found myself staring at an alien couple. Seated facing me in a tiny stone shrine or temple sat an elderly man of about fifty-five, with a long white beard, clad in a white ankle-length cotton garment. Around his neck hung a heavy string of large brown beads which he was idly fingering. Close by his elbow on a small stone ledge seemed a tiny face in some kind of holder. And at his feet, with her back to my gaze, sat a young woman about nineteen in a snow-white fine cotton garment, also ankle-length. Her jet-black hair hung down below her waist in one single, broad braid. It was night. The diminishing chamber was wrapped in thick silence, and a profound peace and attention flowed between the two figures. He appeared to be instructing her. Her face was lifted toward him; her attitude was of alert respect. Who these people might be I had not the remotest notion. But the radiance that emanated from the man was something my young life had never encountered. I have spoken of the devotion and love of my parents. But I was in the presence of love of another order, and such was the difference that the same word can scarcely be applied to both conditions. My heart swelled and tears trickled down. With unaccountable perception I began to ask myself why my parents had such children. Why did they not occupy themselves with significant and mature pastimes? Why were their friends so childish and super- ficial? And what was I doing in this alien Canadian life, anyway? Inundated, almost convulsed with a nostalgic longing, I buried my head beneath the covers and softly wept myself to sleep. Even for the few moments of the vision's duration, it was crystal clear to me that here was real love—boundless, pure, radiant, gentle, all- encompassing, and most of all, entirely free.

And child though I was, I made a passionate resolve to seek out this man one day, when I grew up, and never, never leave him. Then the vision faded and it was some eighteen years until I had occasion to recall it.

Eighteen years later I had another experience. Again I saw the young girl and the man and felt this all- encompassing love. This time the memory was accom- panied by the realization of what the scene I was seeing meant. The young girl was receiving spiritual instruction from a spiritual master. The love I felt was not the ordinary love that I had been accustomed to feeling for my parents or my friends. It was a love of a wholly different order. A voice told me during my second experience that I must search for this man, that although I had known him in another life, he still lived in a new life, as I did today. I recalled the resolution I had made as a child to seek this man, and I renewed it. My search took many years and I traveled the world. I finally found him many years later in New York City. After I had searched the Far East and Europe, how strange it was to find him so close to my home. I recognized him immediately, although his physical resemblance was quite different from what it had been in his previous life when I had been instructed by him. Again in this life he was my spiritual master.

I hesitated to ask him if he too was aware of the fact that we had had a relationship in the distant past. I decided that the best thing to do was simply to tell him of my vision, but not to mention to him that I now realized that it was he I had been seeking. After I had told him of my two experiences, he considered them. He then informed me that the girl I had seen dressed in white had been myself in a past life, and that the man I had seen her with had been himself.

Karmic Connection Remembrances

Karmically connected souls are persons whose karma (actions) have temporarily joined them, until such time as their actions together have been completed. The link between karmically connected individuals is not so highly developed as the bonds between twin souls or soul mates. Karmically connected souls appear to be drawn back together strictly on the basis of their past life relationships, regardless of whether those relationships were good or bad. While I have studied several cases in which karmically connected individuals have not been related, in the majority of cases these individuals appear to reincarnate as family members in several lifetimes.

The following remembrance is an example of a typical karmic family relationship in which two souls reincarnated together again in the same relationship.

John owns a grocery store in a small town in Indiana. He had a remembrance in which he saw a prior relationship with his mother in another life.

My mother and I have always been very close. One night several years ago she died without warning. I was stricken with grief for weeks. I couldn't eat or sleep. I simply didn't care if I lived or died.

It was a cold night in December. I had built a fire in the fireplace, and my wife had gone ahead of me to bed. I was looking into the fire when I heard a loud vibrating noise. It was so loud I couldn't even hear myself think. It got louder and louder and then I felt a presence. I saw my mother standing in front of me in the center of the room. I rubbed my eyes in disbelief. I didn't know what to do; then suddenly I felt a rush of energy pass through me as if someone were shooting jolts of electricity up and down my spinal column. The room faded and I saw I was in a different house. Where my mother had been standing, I now saw a younger woman with brown hair. Then a man walked into the room. He walked over to the woman and kissed her, and then he put on his overcoat and began to leave. I called out to them, but they appeared not to hear me. I was very confused, and, not comprehending, I continued to watch the sequence of events in the room unfold before my eyes.

After the man left, the woman began to straighten up the room. Then she sat down and began to knit. A young boy in pajamas came into the room and approached her. She smiled at him, and he sat down at her feet. A dual sensation filled me. I was seeing the whole scene from a distance, as if I was floating in the air, and at the same time I was seeing through the eyes of the young boy. I saw my mother (the boy's mother) reach out, and I felt her stroke my head. I put my arms around her leg and hugged her. I felt protected and surrounded by her love. I was very tired and closed my eyes. I started to slip off into a dream. Then I found myself back in the air watching the boy and his mother. I stayed watching them for a long time. I knew that I was watching myself and my mother in another life. We had been mother and son before, just as we had been in this life. I was overcome with gratitude that God had allowed us to be together as mother and son in two lifetimes. My sorrow left me. The scene faded and I regained my own body. I was alone in my living room again.

Edna is a clinical psychologist who has a practice in Manhattan. She had a remembrance while she was looking for a house in Brooklyn. She believes the remembrance provided her with information that eventually helped her meet one of her sons from a former lifetime.

I have lived in Brooklyn for the last four years. Last year I began to have visions of myself living in the same area, only in a previous lifetime. The first vision occurred one day when I was looking for a new house to rent. I had been given the key to a house by my real estate agent. I went there and was looking it over when I looked outside the window and saw that the houses across the street were not there; instead there was a lot with trees in it. I walked closer to the window, and as I stared I saw two young boys walking down the street in front of the house. But they were dressed like the boys in the Norman Rockwell paintings. They had on suspenders and knickers. Then a car came down the street—it was an old Ford, the kind my father had when I was a young girl. I drew back from the window and, looking around the living room, saw that everything had changed. The furniture was different, the TV was gone, and it all seemed newer. I looked down at my dress and saw that it too had changed; it went down to the floor. I walked over to a mirror that was hanging where one of the pictures had been and I looked at myself. It wasn't me who was staring back; it was another face, a woman with reddish hair and very dark eyes.

As I stared into her eyes, everything began to get very misty. I felt a wave of light pass through me. It rose from the bottom of my spine until it passed through my head. Everything got foggy for a few minutes, and then I looked around and saw that everything was back to normal; it was exactly as it had been before I had the vision.

Several days later I was speaking with a man who lives down the block who has lived in the neighborhood for over sixty years. Out of curiosity I asked him if he remembered whether there had ever been an empty lot across from that house. He said that yes, there had been, when he was a boy. I asked him about the previous tenants of the house I had looked at. He told me that the house had not been occupied for a number of years. But the last person who had lived there was a man who had inherited the house when his parents had died. I asked him if he remembered what the man's mother had looked like. He described her, and his description was very similar to the face I had seen in the mirror.

My curiosity was aroused, and I decided to do a little research. I found out the owner's name from my real estate agent and was able to contact him. Fortunately he had only moved to another part of Brooklyn. I told him that I just wanted to talk to him about the house and that I would be glad to come to his house if I could. During my visit I asked him if he had any old photos of his family and the house. He showed me some in an old album. One photo of his mother made my hair stand on end; it was the woman I had seen in the mirror. I left his house and returned home. That was the end of my first vision.

After thinking about it, I went back a week later and

visited the man again. I explained all the details of my
experience to him. I was very nervous. I was happy to be
with him, but I was afraid he wouldn't understand me.
We talked for some time and then were silent. He then told
me he believed it was true. He also was feeling close
to me.

That was quite some time ago. We are now the best of
friends. He comes and visits me frequently.

In the following remembrance Wilma, a hairdresser in Salt
Lake City, and her husband Bob, a mining engineer, who had
been members of the same family in a previous lifetime reincarnated together again. But in their current life they have
a different type of relationship.

Falling in love with my second husband was easy to do.
I met him at a dance, and I felt I wanted him to be with
me. Fortunately he felt the same way I did. We were
married after a quick engagement.

The way we related to each other was different from
any way I have been with a man before. It wasn't
only a physical attraction, as it had been for me with my
first husband; I just wanted to be with him. He would
advise me, scold me when I did something wrong, and
encourage me to succeed at all the things I tried to
do. I felt like a little girl with him. I admired him so much,
I wanted to please him and have him be proud of me.
I wanted to be his favorite.

One night we were sitting watching a movie on TV.
He was half reading the paper as he watched. I started to
slip off into another world. Things came into my mind—
landscapes, people—that I did not understand. I looked
over at my husband, but he was changed. He had a long
white beard and glasses. (My husband has no beard or
glasses.) I was shocked at what I saw. I was about to
speak out when I saw that I was different. I was dressed
like a little girl. I understood. Then it went away and
I was back in the present. It was all clear to me. My

husband and I had been with each other in a previous
incarnation. He had been my father and I his daughter.
I understood why we treated each other the way we do.

Unlike twin souls and soul mates who always feel that their
relationship is positive and that it contributes directly to
their growth and happiness, karmically connected persons
do not always feel that they are helpful to each other. Often
their relationship is similar to that of a husband and wife
who no longer love each other but stay together because
they are so used to each other.

In the following remembrance a producer of television
situation comedies narrates his experiences when he encountered a woman he believes he married in a previous
lifetime.

I produce and direct several nationally syndicated
television sit-coms. Two years ago I met and became close
with one of the actresses in one of my shows. We
moved in with each other. At first we were very happy.
Sometimes you can be so involved with another person
that you don't realize the effect she is having upon you. My
friends told me I wasn't acting like my usually carefree
self. I was irritable with the crew and with my actors.
I was moody and depressed and was contemplating
seeing a psychiatrist when I had an experience I find
difficult to believe.

We were working on the set, doing a pilot for a new
show I was trying to syndicate. The show was about a
couple who were happy with each other until they got
married. Their marriage was a loss from the word go.
They divorced and then started to see each other again and
were happy. Then they moved back in with each other and
were miserable again. It was a black comedy I had
written shortly after my girlfriend had moved in with me.
I was so involved with what I was doing that I didn't
even catch on that my subconscious was giving me
a message.

I was thinking about what I could do to give the script
a little more flair when it hit me. I hadn't written this
story about someone who never existed; it was about me
and my girlfriend. A door in my head opened up, and
I saw into the past. I felt a burning or tingling sensation
all around my forehead. It happened so fast that I didn't
miss a line from the rehearsal. I saw that my girlfriend and
I had been husband and wife in America maybe a hundred
or so years ago. We were poor farmers. I managed to get
enough money from my crops to keep us out of debt
each year, but I never got ahead. Our marriage was very
strained. We weren't happy with each other, but I
guess we figured we would stick it out because of the
kids. I had a feeling of emptiness, utter emptiness, the
whole time I was seeing all of this. It all appeared in vivid
three-dimension color pictures.

I reflected on it. I comprehended why my girlfriend
and I had fallen in love with each other—we were used
to each other. It was like an old pair of shoes that feel
good on your feet but you should throw away because they
are worn out. I decided to break up with her, because I
would not allow myself to go through another empty
lifetime like the one I had remembered.

After we broke up I noticed an immediate change in
myself. I felt like someone had taken a great weight
off my shoulders. My friends noticed the change too. They
told me they were glad to see I was back to my usual
happy self. You know, if you had told me this I would
have thought you were crazy. When it happens to you, it's
different; then you have to believe it, because you saw
it yourself.

Twin Births

The birth of twins or triplets poses an interesting question
for the student of reincarnation. If, as the theory of reincarnation postulates, the soul of an individual is capable of
choosing the family it will enter into, then it stands to reason

that a soul can also choose to incarnate with one or more specific souls at the time of birth.

I have interviewed three persons who were born as twins. While this is not a great enough number to make any across-the-board generalizations about the relationships of all twins, I find it interesting to note that all three remembrances indicate that these souls incarnated together to seek revenge on one another for wrongs committed in a past life. In two cases the negative aspect of the relationship carried over from one life to another: neither twin liked the other, and the two tried to have as little to do with each other as possible. In the third case the twins felt they had overcome their problems from their previous life together and were now the best of friends.

The following remembrance recounts the experience of the third set of twins:

My brother and I are identical twins. We look so much alike that when we were in high school we would go on dates together and we could switch places and the girls would never know it. I love my brother very much and he loves me, but we didn't always feel like that. Growing up, my brother and I fought continually. Even when we were very young we would always try to hurt each other or take toys from each other. We had terrible fights over everything, year after year. I think my poor mother wished she had never brought us into the world, we fought so much.

But slowly the way we looked at each other shifted gears. By the time we were in our teens we were able to spend a day with each other without once getting into an argument. By the time we were in high school we went on double dates. We became good friends, much to our mother's happiness.

I found out why it was so difficult for us to get along when we were kids. It came to me one night in a dream. I call it a dream, but it was like no dream I have ever had

before or since. It was so strong and made me understand
something important.

The dream was in another country. My brother and
I were in the dream. We were brothers in this other life.
We were both in love with a very pretty girl with blond
hair. We both wanted to marry her. We fought over her
and became bitter enemies. We swore vengeance on
each other. As things turned out, she married someone else
anyway. That didn't affect our feud. We had nothing
to do with each other for the rest of our lives. Even
at death we did not call for each other.

Incomplete Past Life Relationships

An incomplete past life relationship is a relationship in
which the unexpected death of one of the parties involved
terminates the relationship prematurely. In these cases people
often come back together in another lifetime and complete
the experiences they did not finish in their previous relationship. The following two remembrances are typical of this
type of relationship.

Phillip is an engineering major at the University of Colorado in Boulder. He hopes eventually to design solar heating
devices. He helps to pay his expenses at school by working
part-time in a hardware store.

Phillip met a girl in the store to whom he was very much
attracted. He started dating her regularly and soon fell in
love with her. He had a remembrance in which he saw that
the two of them had been lovers in an earlier life. In the
following segment of his account he describes the nature of
their previous connection.

I was working in the hardware store and met a girl
there who was one of the customers. I asked her out on
a date. We started going steady after a few months. I
liked her, but I can't tell you why: she was not my type
at all. We had very different intercsts. I liked jazz; she

liked classical music. I liked adventure novels; she liked poetry. We had nothing in common. We went with each other for about a year; then we parted. It was a mutual feeling between us. We felt it was time to end it.

The night we broke up we went for a drive out to the lake. We sat there looking into each other's eyes. I was sort of sad that we were breaking up, even though I thought it was the thing to do. I had gotten to like her. I was looking at her eyes when I saw this light circle all around her body. She glowed in the dark. Her face changed, her hair, her body, her clothes. She wasn't the girl who had been sitting on the other side of my car. It was like I was in a trance. I could only watch and witness it. Memories came, all from so long ago. We had been in love before, in another life. I had gone off to war. Before we parted we made a vow that we would be with each other again. I saw something else then. I was killed in the war by a bomb. I wanted to come back to her but I died. I remembered dying and thinking how sad and alone she would be when she heard. Her name was in my mind when I died.

Our vow came true, but it took a long time. We met again and we finished it. I feel that's why it had to end. We finished what we had to finish, and then each of us had to go our own way.

Catherine is the manager of a laundry. She is sixty-two years old and lives in Burlington, Vermont. She had a remembrance in a Catholic church one Sunday that revealed a connection she had had with her son in a previous incarnation.

I have three children, two boys and one girl. I love all my children, but I do have a favorite—my youngest son, David. I would never tell them, but it's true. When I was pregnant with David, I had a vision. I was in church praying on a Sunday. I was praying that my child would be born healthy. I felt dizzy and thought I was passing out. The church went black in my sight. At the other end of the blackness I saw a tiny point of light. It got brighter and brighter, and soon I was surrounded by light. I was flying up above, in the air. My body was in the church still, but I was above it.

I've always felt close to Ireland. I found myself there. It was like I had always pictured it would be. I saw a woman there with her young boy. They were walking down the road carrying food from the town. They came to a sharp curve in the road. The boy was running far ahead of his mother, playing at some kind of game. I saw a man on a horse come round the corner fast. He didn't even have a chance to see the poor lad. He ran him down right there in the road. It was an awful sight to behold. The mother was crying and weeping over her dead son. That's when I felt it. I felt that the woman I was seeing was me. I was sure of it. The boy who died was the boy I was to be having soon. It was plain as day.

This boy has never been a problem to me like the others were. He always wants to please me. Even when he was a little one he hardly cried at all. When he did it was because he wanted to be with me.

He came back to me from beyond death. Our love was that strong. I do believe in reincarnation now. It's true. We don't go to heaven when we die. We come back here, at least for a while.

BEYOND BIRTH AND DEATH

Birth and death are inseparable. Birth precedes death, death succeeds birth. What we need to connect both birth and death is Life. Strangely enough, this Life existed before our birth, it exists between our birth and death, and will exist after death, stretching its far-flung arms into Eternity, Infinity and Immortality.

Sri Chinmoy: *Beyond Within*

Changed Attitudes

The most striking changes in a person's attitudes after a past life remembrance have to do with the issues of death and dying. For most persons the subject of death is distasteful. They deal with it only when it is brought directly into their lives through the loss of a friend or a loved one, or when they are near the brink of death themselves. In my experience most persons in our society choose to avoid the subject either by feigning a lack of interest in it or by saying, "I'll worry about it when the time comes." If you are a curious individual like me who only becomes more interested in a subject when someone tries to avoid it, people tell you that you are morbid or that you have a preoccupation with things that are "best left up to God." But people who have had a past life remembrance not only are willing to discuss death and dying; they are actually eager to do so. When I asked these individuals if they had always been interested in the subject, their reply was "No." Most people reported that before their past life remembrance they thought that death was a "scary," "morbid" or "unnatural" topic for discussion. But after their past life experience, death was not a subject to be avoided but one to be looked at in a positive and joyful way.

Twenty-five people reported that their remembrance gave them an entirely new view of life and death. Fifty-one said it served to change or modify their understanding of life and death. In the remainder of cases there were significant changes in the people's attitudes toward life and death, but they did not ascribe the changes entirely to their remembrance. They felt that their remembrance was the first step in redefining their understanding, but their total reevaluation of life and death was also subject to other experiences they had after their remembrance.

The most common change in attitude is the acceptance of death as simply another stepping-stone in the endless journey of life. Many of the persons I spoke with expressed the idea that death is a sort of holiday that gives them a rest before they come back to another life on this earth.

Jane first saw scenes from her past life in Greece while babysitting. Several years later she visited Greece during a college vacation and had a second remembrance of her Grecian past life. She told me that before her remembrance she had been afraid of death, but that since then her feelings had changed.

Now I feel as if death is just another step I will someday take, the same way I knew that one day I would come of age. I know now that the time will come when I will die, and it will come just as naturally as aging or growing. It's not a step off the end of the world; it's just as concrete and real a step as the step to be born.

Before my past life vision I had a fear of death. Actually it wasn't even so much a fear as that I had no knowledge of it—I didn't comprehend it. In my youth, death wasn't a reality to me. And then as I grew older and saw relatives dying and so on, when I thought how my soul would one day leave my body lying there, the fear began. I wondered, just where does my soul go? It was not knowing that made me afraid. But now that I know what happens, I could never be afraid.

After John had his medieval remembrance, his views on life and death were totally changed.

The best part of my reincarnation vision was the change it produced in me. I have never been afraid of my own death. But the thought of all my family and my friends dying made me depressed. I looked at life and it seemed so full. On a spring day the sun was shining, the flowers were in bloom, the air was sweet and clean, the birds were singing. To think that all that would end and die and that's it—well, I could never feel good about life. It seemed like a cruel joke. I could not enjoy my life because I always knew that no matter how good or how wonderful anything I experienced was, it would eventually come to an end in death. Then nothing would matter. No matter what I accomplished, who I loved, what I felt, it would all come to nothing.

My feelings have changed. I know now that I wasn't looking at life right. Seeing the other times I lived, I became aware that it doesn't end. It's all part of a beautiful cycle. We are born, we live, we die, and we are born again. It's even in the seasons: spring, summer, fall, winter; and then in the spring life is reborn.

It simply comes down to the fact that I didn't trust God. If I would really let myself go and had faith in God, then I would not worry. I would know that He is always there, guiding and protecting me, whether I am aware of

His presence or not. He created me and gave me life—His life. He is not going to take it away.

Harry told me that the idea of death used to give him "the creeps." But since his remembrance he no longer has any fear of death.

I never liked to even think about death before.
Whenever I thought of death I felt empty. I would think, "My God, it will all end, and my life will be over." Ever since I saw my past life, I don't mind talking about death or thinking about it. Why should I mind?
Death is not the end.

In his story *Captain Stormfield's Visit to Heaven*, Mark Twain describes the after-death adventures of a sea captain. Before Captain Stormfield died he had a typical conception of heaven. He imagined that when he arrived, he would be greeted by Saint Peter at the pearly gates. He would then receive a halo and wings and would spend the rest of his existence on a cloud, playing celestial music. But upon arriving in heaven shortly after his death, Captain Stormfield was surprised to see millions of different types of beings and creatures passing through hundreds of gates into heaven. He finally found the gate for humans and was issued a harp, a pair of wings and a halo. He found a vacant cloud and played his harp for a few hours and then began to be bored. Finally he climbed down from his cloud and went back to return his harp, wings and halo. As he did so, he saw hundreds of other people doing the same thing. All had thought that heaven was a place where they would sit on a cloud and play a harp. When they arrived in heaven they were given what they expected so that they wouldn't be upset. But once they finally realized that heaven was far different from that, they threw away their preconceived ideas about it and started to explore what was really there.

The people I have questioned about their past life remembrances have gone through a similar awakening. Before their remembrance many of them had a preconceived notion that heaven was a physical place where their souls would go after death. They did not have a clear idea what they would do there. Like Captain Stormfield, they thought they would simply put on a halo and sit on a cloud for eternity. But their remembrance totally changed their ideas about an afterlife, as in the case of Allen, who feels that his Egyptian remembrance provided him with an entirely new understanding of what lies beyond death.

> Before, I saw heaven as an escape. Sometimes life on
> earth is pretty rotten. I guess I thought heaven would
> be a place to rest. There would be peace there. But I
> was wrong. I experienced heaven when I had the scenes
> from my past lives. I was in complete joy and peace. I
> saw that heaven is not a place you can go to after one life.
> You live many lives on this earth. Heaven is how you
> feel; it's inside you.

Sal owns a delicatessen on the East Side of Manhattan. He told me that his remembrance changed his understanding both of God and of life after death.

> I saw my God was a God of mercy. He won't send some
> to hell and some to heaven. He gives us hundreds of lives,
> hundreds of chances to learn. I think everybody goes
> to God eventually. How could a God of love have it
> any other way? When I saw my lives on a chain, I said to
> myself, I understand it all now. I have lived before and
> will again. Heaven—I'll get there. But first I have to
> become worthy of it. I can't do it in one life; it's too short.
> In hundreds, thousands, maybe. But in one? Impossible.

Althea is a music teacher who lives in Birmingham, Alabama. Since her remembrance she feels that she has become more conscious not only of her past lives, but also of the people and events in her current lifetime.

Imagine that you have awakened from a dream. In your dream you were in a hollow land. Everything was shadows. You saw figures moving in and out of the darkness, but you couldn't exactly see them because it was so dark. Then you woke up. You rubbed your eyes and saw that the world wasn't dark and filled with shadows. It was filled with light and with people and beautiful things. That's how I felt. My past lives woke me up. I was living in shadows before it happened. Then I became aware of so much more. It's not vague at all; it's perfectly easy to see, once you get a new view on things.

Leonard also feels that his past life vision has given him a new perspective on his life.

One of the best courses I took in college was in philosophy. The professor had us do a paper about the nature of ourselves. I remember writing the paper and formulating all the ideas I had had about who and what I was as I then conceived of myself. I wrote about my likes and dislikes, things I believed in or thought were wrong, and so on. The point is that I saw myself in terms of my ideas and feelings about the world and the people and things that exist in it. My visions into my previous incarnations changed all of those perceptions and ideas. If I were to write that paper today, it would be entirely different. I would write that I no longer see myself as a person who is born and dies, and who exists for a short while in between, is happy or sad, and fails or succeeds. I see myself now more in terms of thousands of lifetimes. I am more conscious that I am developing in each lifetime toward something higher; I am growing and improving. Death is not my end, and birth is not my beginning. What happens to me in this one life is not that big a concern to me. Of course I care; certainly I do. But it's sort of like the old adage about not seeing the forest for the trees, if you know what I mean. When I used to think that I lived only this life, everything that

happened in this one life was really important. I was only
seeing the trees. I would get hung up on my little problems
and difficulties because they seemed so all-encompassing
to me. Today I know I have many, many lives to lead.
Each one is different and unique. Today I see that the
"trees," my problems, aren't so important. I cannot be
troubled by the little things in this life.

One of the most significant changes in attitude that people
reported lay in their conception of their soul. Over seventy
percent of the people who had remembrances felt that they
"experienced" their soul, and they are now firmly convinced
that it exists Twenty percent said that they feel there is a
part of them that will live on after death, although they
would not necessarily use the term "soul" to describe it. The
remaining ten percent are still unsure as to whether they have
a soul but are convinced that they are connected with an
eternal "spirit" that will exist beyond their own death.
    Pamela Cohen feels that she experienced her soul during
her remembrance.

    I was very worried about death before. I thought that
    one day I would die and that would be the end. Death is
    something I tried to avoid thinking about. I didn't
    know how to deal with it. Nothing could be more
    frightening to me than to think that I would end, that I
    wouldn't exist anymore.
    My experience changed all that. After seeing my past
    lives I realized that I can't die. My soul is immortal. And
    it's not just my soul that is immortal; everything is
    immortal. Everything has a spirit which resides within it,
    and if you can see that, then there is nothing to fear.
    I saw the eternal spirit inside myself and saw that it has
    been a part of me since the beginning of time, all through
    my lives, and will be with me forever.

Alexis's remembrance of his death in the Civil War gave
him a new vision of his soul.

I never had a clear idea of what my soul was or did, although I was pretty sure I had one. I knew I had to come from somewhere and that when I died, a part of me would survive. But I really felt my soul during my experience. It wasn't an idea, it was the real me. I could see it moving from life to life; it didn't die.

Harry states:

I have never believed in the soul. I could never feel it or see it, so why should I think it's there? During my visions of my other lives, I realized I did have something like that. It's a part of me that lives forever. It's not my personality or anything like that. It's not male or female either. I guess you could call it a soul, or spirit, or anything you want.

Telling Others

After the completion of a past life remembrance, the first reaction of most people is to try to share their experience with others. Their situation is similar to that of a person who took a trip to a foreign country which none of his friends had visited. While he was there he saw sights, heard sounds and had a variety of experiences which changed his whole outlook on life. His experience was so powerful that upon his return he wanted to share it with others. He anticipated that everyone whom he would tell about his trip would be happy that he had seen and done so many wonderful things and learned so much. But to his surprise he discovered that those friends with whom he shared his experiences did not believe he had actually had them. What is more, they greeted his experiences with apathy, hostility or fear. Hoping that someone else would understand, he tried telling other friends and members of his family. But the reactions were always the same; people either could not understand what he described to them or simply expressed no interest.

The difficulties facing a person who tries to share his past life remembrance with someone else are even more complex than those in my analogy. The intensely personal quality of a remembrance makes it difficult for even the most articulate person to express it in terms that will make sense to someone who has not had such an experience. But what poses an even greater threat to sharing it is the total fear and disbelief that is ingrained in our Western culture regarding out-of-the-body phenomena. While science has given tremendous technological benefits to our society, it has also brought with it a very narrow view of life. The scientist is primarily interested in observable and quantifiable phenomena. He feels that the existence of anything that cannot be tested or measured is purely hypothetical. While it is understandable that a scientist must use this perspective in studying physical phenomena, it is a fallacy to assume that this one perspective is suitable for exploring all of life. The physical sciences are still in their infancy, but because they have come to play such a dominant role in our lives, we invest them with Godlike attributes which perhaps they do not have.

The question of the limitations of the scientific perspective versus the subjective way of seeing things has been debated since the time of Plato. While it is certainly not necessary to choose one or the other, we must, in a technologically top-heavy world, consider the essential validity of our own experiences. The microscope and the telescope are wonderful inventions, and the age of knowledge they have ushered in has changed all of our lives; but as any religious or philosophically minded person knows, there are areas of reality that these scientific instruments cannot penetrate.

Given the general closed-mindedness of our culture to out-of-the-body phenomena, it is easy to understand the predicament of an individual who has just had a past life remembrance. He finds it difficult to articulate his experiences, not because they were in any way vague or uncertain, but because our language does not have an adequate vocabulary to describe them. Even if he can explain them to others, the first reaction of the average person who is unfamiliar with the subject is to disbelieve and to reject the experiences as the products of someone's imagination.

After listening to enough doubts about their past life remembrances, many people begin to question the validity of their own experiences. In this sense the doubts of others are infectious, and it is only a remarkably strong individual who can rise above them and still believe in his visions of a past life. Very often the family and friends of someone who has had a past life remembrance will apply social and even economic pressure to make him "forget" his experiences or at least stop telling people about them.

The following statements were made by four people who felt the necessity of sharing their past life remembrances with those around them in the hope of communicating what they considered to be the most remarkable experience of their lives.

Bill is an electronics technician for a company in Dallas. He had a remembrance of a former lifetime in which he was a monk in southern Europe during the twelfth century. He told his friends about it, expecting them to be fascinated by his experience. Instead, they ridiculed his story.

The day after I had my experience, I could hardly get to work fast enough to tell a few of the guys I worked with about what happened to me. I figured they would be as amazed as I had been. At lunch that day I cornered two of my friends and told them. I knew what I was saying probably sounded kind of far-out, but I was sure that they thought I was pretty sound and level-headed and I wasn't going to go off the deep end or nothing like that. Well, first they laughed 'cause they thought I was putting them on or something. But then I got mad—you know, like that fella in that movie, *Close Encounters of the Third Kind.* I remember how he had seen flying saucers and he tried to tell his wife. She just looked at him like he was out of it, like he was crazy. Well that's how my friends treated me. They humored me. I got really pissed

off and walked away from them; I mean they were so
narrow-minded. I tried to tell some other people, but the
same thing happened. They said I was dreaming or
that I had had too much to drink. I tried to tell them that
I wasn't drinking or dreaming, that I saw what I saw. But
they couldn't understand. Not only that, they didn't want
to understand. Anything in this world that causes them
to think about what they don't know, they can't seem
to handle. I finally gave up. What the hell, I had the
experience and I know it was for real. The thing is, there's
no way to prove it. And it's too bad. Not so much for
me—I had the experience—but for them. I mean they
have no idea what life is about, not really; they just
think they do.

Ahmed is a professional basketball player. Like many of
the persons I spoke with, he told me that at first he was afraid
to tell anyone about his experience because he feared everyone would think he was crazy. But after keeping silent about
it for several weeks, he finally felt the necessity to share it
with someone. He felt that if anyone would believe his story,
it would be his wife. But her reaction to his account was far
different from what he expected.

I told the story to my wife. She seemed very interested
when I told her I had seen her and myself in a past life
together in Africa. She told me that she had always
been intrigued by that part of the world. Then she
changed her feelings. I can only guess that she must have
talked to some of her friends and they told her it all
sounded crazy. She even became hostile. I tried to mention
it to our oldest daughter, and my wife told me it was wrong
to tell her a lot of "fairy tales." She even threatened to
leave me if I talked about it anymore. It was as if I
had committed some kind of crime. Can you believe it?

Rita is a secretary for a law firm in Seattle, Washington.
She was very excited by her remembrance and wanted to

share her revelations with her family and friends. But she was so discouraged by their reactions that she gave up trying to tell anyone else about her experience.

I thought there was something wrong with me; I started to believe that I had gone out of my mind or something. When you told me that other people had seen past lives like I had, I felt so much better. I knew then I wasn't crazy at all. But when I first told my family, it was a different story. After I saw my past life I was so excited. My life changed with remembering my past lifetimes. I wanted to tell everyone. I felt like I had discovered the greatest thing in the world. I was never a person who likes to keep good things to herself. If I find something good—a new food or a better way of dieting or something—I tell all my friends. I would hope that they would tell me when they find something really good. That's how we help each other. Well, my friends all thought I was out of my mind, except for one who I found out has always been into psychic things. My husband couldn't have cared less one way or the other, and my mother told me that I should go and talk to our priest. Well, I did. I thought if anyone would be able to tell me what had happened to me, he would. But talking to him was a waste of time; he treated me like a child who was telling him about some dream she had had.

Mary shared her remembrance—of a life as a Mother Superior in a convent in France—with her friends at the university where she teaches. She was surprised that they considered her remembrance only a product of her imagination.

I must admit I was rather shocked by the reactions of the people I told. What bothered me the most was not what they said but the expressions on their faces. They listened to all I told them, and some friends even told me

how remarkable it all was. But I could see in their eyes
and in their faces how they really felt. I immediately
thought of Christ and Moses and how difficult it must
have been for them to try to tell their people about the
higher spiritual realities. I really can identify with Christ
now; I never really understood what He was saying
when He said, "Father, forgive them, for they know not
what they do." But they don't know; people have no
idea. They don't see; they haven't had this type of
experience. I can't blame them for that, I suppose. But
they are so blind. One of my so-called friends even
told me that I had better not talk about it at work because
they would probably think I was a weirdo and fire me.
Can you imagine that? This may be the twentieth century,
but people's minds are still back in the Dark Ages.

Confirmation

One of my concerns throughout my study of reincarnation
has been to try to verify any information that suggests that
the process of reincarnation actually exists. The recurrence
of similar phenomena in all the past life remembrances presented to me, coupled with the striking similarities between
these remembrances and the descriptions of the death and
rebirth process as depicted in the *Tibetan Book of the Dead*
and other Far Eastern books on reincarnation, lend a certain
amount of credibility to the theory of reincarnation. But in
several of the remembrances there has been more direct information that reincarnation is not simply a theory but an
actuality.

The information in these cases is of two kinds: (1) information that is supported by verifiable facts; and (2) information that has conclusively demonstrated to the individual
who had the remembrance that his experience was genuine.
While the first type of information will possibly have a
greater impact on the average person's assessment of the
credibility of reincarnation, the information in the second

category, while admittedly subjective, is just as noteworthy and important.

The majority of remembrances have not lent themselves to historical verification either because the remembrances revealed information about past lifetimes that took place hundreds or thousands of years ago or because the remembrances did not reveal enough specific information (such as a person's name or address in a past lifetime). But the fact that the phenomena and their sequence were identical both in the verifiable accounts and in those that were not verifiable suggests that all the accounts are of the same nature and are therefore credible.

At the request of the persons who gave me the following two accounts, I have altered the names and locations.

Mary is a real estate broker who lives in Tampa, Florida. She and her sister took her son and daughter on a vacation to Acapulco. While they were there her son, Charlie, had a remembrance of his most recent past lifetime.

We had a guide who picked us up in Monterrey and took us into the different areas of Mexico. I had my four-year-old son with me. While in Acapulco we went to see the divers; they dive off the cliffs about every four hours into the water. This was the evening dive, when they take the torch and dive with it. It was quite impressive, and Charlie, my son, was quite awed by it all. He did not speak the whole time, except at one point when his view was obstructed and he was unable to see it.

When we were leaving, Charlie said to me, as if he were in a trance, "I died once." I thought he had said, "I dived once," and I said, "You dived once? When did you dive?" and he repeated, "I died once." And I said, "Well, when did you die, Charlie?" He said, "I died once, and it hurt." Immediately I sensed that something special was going on. He seemed to have lost touch with what was around him physically; he seemed to be actually seeing something that was not where we were. My sister

was with me also, and she became aware of this
immediately. While we were walking to the car, I
realized that he was seeing the past, and I thought I
had better ask him any questions about it immediately. I
asked, "How did you die?" He said, "I was hit; I was hit
in the leg, and it hurt; it hurt bad." And while he was
telling us, he was going through this hurt. All of his
muscles were tense, and he was almost crying. I could see
that he was in pain. I asked him how he got hurt, and
he said he had been on a ship in a big war. "What big
war?" I asked. He answered, "The big war of 1942." I
asked him where he lived, and he said on the ship. I said,
"No, before you were on the ship—where did you live
then?" He said, "Up there," and he pointed. And I asked,
"Up where?" He said, "Up in California." I said, "Well,
what was your name?" And he said, "My name was James
Kellow." And I said, "Krestan—do you say it that way?"
And he said, "No, Kellow." I had a little trouble understanding exactly how he was pronouncing the name.
Then my sister interrupted. She said, "Well, how did you
die, Charlie?" He said, "I was on a raft, and there were
three fellas with me. One of them fell off, and the other
one died on the raft." When the raft finally landed on the
ground on a beach, he told us, he pulled the other fella
off, and then he said, "After I pulled him off, then I died.
And it hurt."

Then my sister said, "Well how did it happen, Charlie?"
And he said, "Well, it was just all of a sudden; it was just
sounds and big explosions and a lot of colors, and every-
body was screaming. It was bad, it was bad."

We got it out of him that he was an officer, because I
said, "You were down in the ship," and he said "No," like
he was indignant at the thought that he was an enlisted
man. He said, "I was an officer." I asked him if he was in
his twenties or thirties. He said that he was in his
twenties. I asked him if he was married and he said,
"No." I said, "Were you in love?" And he said, "Yes, I

was in love. I would have married her if I had lived." He
told us that he didn't have brothers or sisters, that he was
an only child, and that his mother and father lived in
California. And I said, "Where in California?" He said,
"San Francisco." And I said, "Do they live in a house,
Charlie?" And he said, "Yes, they live in a house, and
it's a big house, and they were sad—they were real sad—
but I just died. I couldn't help it; I just died." He told
us that his first name had been James. I said, "Did they
call you a nickname?" And he said, "James, and they
called me James." I asked him if he was drafted, and he
said, "No, I chose the navy. I wanted to be a navy officer."
And then he got on the light side, and I could tell he was
coming out of it. I asked him what ship he was on, and
I thought he said he was on the *Alabama*, but I wasn't
sure. He had trouble saying the word.

After we left Mexico I went to Mobile, Alabama; I had
heard that that was where the *Alabama* was. I went
aboard and talked with the commander, and he happened
to be the commander that was on the ship during the
war. He has since retired and is maintaining it as a museum
in Alabama. He let me look at the list, and there were
several Jameses but no James Kellow. The Commander
told me he thought I had it mixed up with the *Arizona*,
because a lot of times those two ships were confused.
He said that the *Alabama* never took a direct hit, but the
Arizona did, and I should check the list of that ship.

But before we left we took Charlie on board the ship.
Charlie had never been on a big navy ship before, but he
knew everything about that ship, just like an experienced
officer would; he knew what holds and doors to go through
to get where he wanted to go and how to get through
them. He'd take his hands and scoot himself through
them just like a sailor does.

Several months later I was able to get a copy of the
Arizona's personnel list, and there it was in black and white
—James Kellow, and he had come from San Francisco.

I realized then that Charlie had been saying that he was on the *Arizona,* not the *Alabama.* Now I had got into this thing so deep it had sort of become an obsession. I decided to go to San Francisco and see his parents and find out what I could. But before going there I thought to myself, "If someone came to me and had any evidence that they had my son whom I had raised, loved, and cared for and who had died some years before, then I would do everything in my power to try and get my son back, or to at least be with him as much as I could." Well, if I went to San Francisco and saw Charlie's parents, I ran the risk that they would start bothering Charlie, and I didn't think it was right to disrupt a child's life like that. He wouldn't know what to think, or who his parents were. So I have decided to wait until Charlie is a little older and then I will give him the information and he can go visit them if he wants to.

After Mary related her story to me, I made an attempt to validate her information. I was able to obtain a copy of the *Arizona*'s personnel list and confirmed that there was an officer on board named James Kellow at the time the ship was attacked and sunk. Further research of navy records revealed that James and another member of the crew had escaped on a raft. Both of their bodies were later found on an island that was some distance from the site where the *Arizona* had gone down.

The following remembrance occurred to Phillip, a writer who lives in Venice, California.

I first met Anne outside of Malibu. I was looking for a small street off the coast road and had turned down another road in hopes of meeting someone I could ask for directions. I drove by a car that was parked on a corner. There was a girl sitting in the car, so I pulled over at the next corner and hopped out of my car and walked back to her.

We both smiled as we met. It was a beautiful sunny day, and I was glad to find that I was in the presence of an attractive girl. I asked her for directions, and she told me she didn't know anything about the area either. She lived in Monterey and had only come to Malibu to attend a psychology seminar.

After that we began to small-talk. She told me she was about to graduate from school in Arizona where she had been majoring in psychology. On an impulse I asked her if she wanted to take a ride with me to a church I was trying to find. She agreed and we got in my car and left.

We found the church without too much trouble. Getting out of the car, we walked around the grounds. It was a beautiful place. There were two main buildings and three small chapels. I was particularly fascinated by the little lake they had on the grounds. A flock of black swans were swimming in it. I had never seen black swans before, and I pointed them out to Anne.

We went into one of the small chapels and sat in silence. The whole time, I was very aware of this girl. It seemed very natural that we were together. I didn't really think about the fact that I had just met her.

We left the church and went to the beach. We walked along the shore together, talking about this and that. We took our shoes off and ran down the beach for a mile or more. Then we collapsed on the sand and watched the ocean.

We stayed together until late afternoon; then I had to return to Los Angeles and she to Monterey. But I told her that I would be visiting friends in Monterey the next weekend, and I gave her the phone number where I would be staying and told her to give me a call if she wanted to. She also gave me her number and the two of us parted.

I had forgotten her, and it was a surprise to me when she called. I was in Monterey; it was the next weekend.

l told her to come over, and I had my friend give her instructions over the phone. She arrived about a half hour later.

We both felt a little awkward. It was as if there was something we both wanted to express but didn't know how or what. There didn't seem to be any reason why the two of us should be so drawn to each other. We were very different types of people. We sat and talked for a while. I spoke quite honestly with her, telling her how I felt, and she said she felt the same way. After an hour we parted. She was returning to Arizona a few days later and told me she would write to me.

I didn't hear from Anne again for about five months. Then, late one night, I woke up to the ringing of the phone. At first I didn't realize who she was. Then it all came back to me. We talked for about half an hour. The whole time I felt so good. My mind was very clear, and I had a happy and comfortable sensation pulsing through my body. We agreed that we had to get together at some future time but we didn't know quite when. We both agreed that we would see each other but that it wasn't something we had to rush. We both had the feeling that we couldn't avoid each other even if we had wanted to; we felt it was destined that we would meet again.

After I had hung up the phone, I saw a past life in which Anne and I had been together. The pictures were scattered at first. I saw farms, sheep, fences and that kind of thing. Then I saw a woman dressed in one of those long peasant dresses. She was walking across the field toward me. She walked up to me and handed me some flowers. I took her arm, and the two of us strolled through the field together. I recognized that it was Anne in another life.

We returned to our car. It was an old one, the kind I have seen in museums. We got in the car and went off down the road.

Her name came to me then: it was Martha, Martha

Williams. I was a minister and she was a close friend of
mine. We were out driving together on a Sunday afternoon
in Colorado.

The vision of us in the car was replaced by other
pictures. I saw myself giving a sermon in front of a large
congregation. I was older now. My orientation shifted
from looking at myself to being inside of myself and
looking out at the crowd. There were thousands of people
there. I was preaching to a huge crowd. It was evening
and we were outside. I could hear the sound of my voice
moving up and down as I changed my intonation. I could
hear the echoes of my voice in the distance through
the speaker system. The stadium was lit by torches and a
few electric lights. I could smell the oily smell of the
torches; it reminded me of the smell of turpentine.

Speaking to the crowd about sin and repentance, I
could feel the presence of the Holy Spirit moving through
me. The people in the crowd were moved by what I
was saying. It was a scene right out of *Elmer Gantry*.
Then the scene shifted and I was someplace else.

I was with Anne again, but this time we were not alone.
There was another woman there—my wife. I was telling
my wife that I was in love with Anne. My wife was crying,
but I was telling her I had to leave her, that I felt it was
God's will that I should be with Anne.

Another scene appeared to me after that. I was alone
in the desert, and I was praying. I felt the power of God
moving through me and lifting me. I saw lives, hundreds
of my lives before. And I felt that God was showing me,
telling me that I was to work for Him. I had been a
spiritual person in almost all of my lives. I was called to
do the work of God and to bring Him into the lives of
people around me. I only wished to be humble and pure
enough to receive Him into my heart and to be allowed
to serve Him. I saw at that time that I would be brought
even closer to Him in my next life.

I saw that I was with Anne again after that. We left

the country and were missionaries in China. We lived there for many years. Both of us had studied and learned the language very well, and we were doing whatever we could to serve the poor and indigent people. We were both acting as teachers, doctors, and ministers to those poor people. The poverty and suffering we saw was incredible. We traveled through many countries and did all we could, but the task was overwhelming.

The last scenes that I witnessed are burned in my mind forever. We were on a boat headed back to America. The Japanese had invaded China and had killed many of our friends. We had some of the orphaned children with us, thinking we could find homes for them in America.

The captain of our small boat sighted a Japanese ship, and we tried to make a run for it. I knew it was hopeless, and I prayed that we would be delivered. We were shelled, and many of the people on the boat were badly hurt or killed. Then the ship came alongside us and we were boarded.

The rest is hard for me to tell. I become upset when I think about it. They took all of the women who were left and raped them in front of us. Anne was among them. Then they killed the women and the children. I saw the one who had raped and killed Anne, and I swore vengeance against him. They took me and the rest of the men inside the boat and tied us up. I overheard one of them say that they were taking us somewhere for forced labor. I could only try to feel that God was working with me and that His will was being done. I prayed most of the time we were on the boat that I would understand God's ways and wouldn't lose faith in Him no matter what happened to me.

We managed to get away that night. One of the men untied himself and undid the ropes that bound the rest of us. We didn't have any weapons, and I knew that we would probably all die, but I felt it was better to die fighting than to lead a life of slavery.

We attacked and killed the ship's watches. I got one of their guns and we went looking for the rest. Somebody heard us and sounded an alarm. In minutes the whole ship was crawling with the Japanese.

I ran into one of the passageways. Standing right in front of me was the Jap who had killed Anne. I didn't give him time to do anything; I just grabbed him around the throat and started to choke him. I don't know why, but I didn't use the gun; I wanted to do it with my own hands. I killed him in a matter of minutes. Then I left him there and went to look for the others.

They forced us to the back of the ship, but we kept fighting. I got hold of one of the deck machine guns and started firing at them. I killed a lot of them, and after a while I felt a cool burning sensation in my shoulder and I looked down and saw that I had been shot. The blood was oozing out on my blue shirt.

A fire had started on the ship. I heard an explosion and was thrown off my feet into the air. I was in the water, swimming, but I knew I wasn't going to make it. I found a box that was floating and hung on to it.

I floated for a long time. I kept thinking that I couldn't hold on any longer, but I somehow did. It was dark and I couldn't see any of the others. I hung on that way all night long.

The next day I was alone. I was afraid of sharks but none came. The sun was burning down on me and I was thirsty, but I couldn't drink the water. I saw a boat in the distance. I was afraid they would miss me, but they came. They took me on board and tried to help. They were Chinese.

I managed to recover and make my way out of the Orient. I went to Australia and stayed there for a time. Then I went on to England and finally back to America.

I started to preach again and did so for six or seven months until I got very sick. I had been weakened by my ordeal in the Orient. I died not long after that.

After that everything came back to normal. I was convinced that I had been with Anne in another life. I couldn't sleep after that so I stayed up all night. The next morning I started to put together some ideas on how I could see whether it was all true.

I remembered our names from our former lives. I started with the town we had lived in while we were in Colorado. After all kinds of checking I found out that a young man by the name of Walter Morris had been a minister there during the 1930s. I traced his movements in one or two places. He had become a well-known revivalist preacher and then had left this country to become a missionary. The information at this point is sketchy, since any records of his activities in China were destroyed during the war. But I talked with some of his relatives and they confirmed most of the things I saw, including his being taken prisoner by the Japanese, his journeys to Australia and England, his return to the United States, and his death. But I didn't find any mention of a Martha Williams in any of the records, nor did any of his relatives know anything about her. I began to wonder if maybe the whole thing wasn't crazy. I didn't understand it.

I had just about given up when I got a phone call from a Mrs. Cowley. She told me that she was informed by some of her relatives that I was seeking information about her father, and she wondered if she could help me. This totally threw me, because I didn't see anything that would indicate that I had ever had a daughter in that life. I asked her if I could come and visit her to talk to her about her father, and she agreed.

I took a plane to South Carolina to visit Mrs. Cowley. She was a very pleasant woman, but I didn't feel I knew her in any way. I told her before I recounted my story that I was a sane, rational person who had had an experience I didn't understand. I didn't know what the experience was all about and I was just trying to figure it all out. I didn't want her to think I was out of my mind or anything like that.

I told her the story from beginning to end. She didn't betray any emotion throughout the story. When I was finished I was sure she was convinced that I was crazy. I calmly waited to be asked to leave. Then she reached out and took my hand into hers. She held it and didn't say a word.

She told me that everything I had said about her father was true. He had left her mother before she was born for another woman named Martha. When Walter had left, neither he nor his wife knew she was pregnant; the child must have been conceived just before he left her.

She had never met her father. Her mother had told her about him but felt very bitter toward him and had never made any attempt to contact Walter and tell him that he had a child. Walter had evidently written his wife and sent her money, but she never responded to any of his letters, although she had saved them all and read through them until they were almost worn out. Mrs. Cowley told me she grew up hating her father for abandoning both herself and her mother. It was only after she had been informed of her father's death that she had felt any emotion for him at all. She went to his funeral (her mother had died five years earlier) and cried. Then she had gone home to her own husband and children and resolved to forget all about the father she had never met.

It was growing late in the afternoon. We sat in silence, looking at each other, wondering if it could be true. Then she asked me if I would like to see the letters her father had sent her mother. She had saved them and had them in a chest with some other personal items that had belonged to her mother.

She gave me the letters. They had been folded and unfolded so many times that they were falling apart. There were dozens of them. Evidently Walter Morris had been a prolific letter writer and had sent his wife the details of all of his adventures.

I read the descriptions of his life and was completely dumfounded. His preaching career, life in the Orient, everything had been the way I had seen it. But what interested me the most were his descriptions of Martha. He described how hard she worked with the sick and the poor, and I could perceive the deep love and respect this man had for her.

Our interview came to a close. I thanked her very much and asked her if I could keep one of the letters. She said of course I could; they were my letters anyway. I didn't know what to say so I thanked her again and left.

After speaking with Phillip, I was able to meet separately with Mrs. Cowley. She confirmed the facts that Phillip had related in his remembrance. Mrs. Cowley also allowed me to examine the letters Walter Morris had written to his wife. They provided the same information that Phillip had seen in his remembrance.

When a person's remembrance makes clear to him why he has specific attitudes, talents, interests or emotional responses that are otherwise inexplicable, this information becomes proof for him that his remembrance was real. Elizabeth Lok had a past life remembrance in which she saw several gentlemen she believes were her relatives in a previous life in Spain.

After my vision of my life in Spain a number of things became very clear to me. I have always been moved by Spanish music. I had been particularly fascinated by El Greco's art and by Moorish Spain. When I was a youth I had been utterly delighted by Spanish dancing. My first studies in Spanish had been a total delight to me. I found the words absolutely entrancing. After I realized that I had lived in Spain in a past life and had spoken Spanish before, I felt compelled to become thoroughly reacquainted with it. I found my study very easy; it was more of a remembering process. The cadences of Spanish

speech were so familiar to me that "learning" it was not
a chore but a delight.

Sam is an economics major at the University of Maine. In
the following account he details a remembrance in which he
saw himself as a concert pianist in a past life:

It was a hot summer night and I was bored. I had
walked around the college where I live looking for something to do, but the place was dead. I walked into one of
the dorm lounges and sat down at a piano. I fooled around
for a couple of minutes trying to pick out an Elton John
song. I have never played the piano or taken music lessons.
But as I was sitting there I started to really play. My
hands seemed to take over as if they knew what they were
doing without my helping them. I played songs by Bach,
Beethoven and Vivaldi. While I played, pictures began
to flash before my eyes. I saw a man dressed in tails
playing a piano in front of hundreds of people. Whenever
he would stop playing, the audience would applaud like
wild. I had the feeling that everything I was seeing was in
Europe. Later, after the concert, I saw the pianist leave the
stage and go to his dressing room. A beautiful woman was
waiting there to meet him. I saw that she was just one
of many women he was romantically involved with. Then
I saw him playing other concerts all over Europe. I
gradually understood that I was him—in another life,
I mean. All the time I was seeing this, I was playing
classical pieces on the piano. Finally the visions quit
coming and I stopped playing. My hands and fingers really
hurt. I looked at my watch and saw that I had been
playing for over two hours. The music I played was
completely recognizable, and I had never really touched
a piano before in my life.

I must say I have always loved classical music. Ever
since I was a little kid I have felt very good when I
listened to it. I have always especially loved
unaccompanied piano music.

Since I had the experience of seeing myself as a pianist,

I have tried to play the piano a couple of times. I find
I can play pieces of music spontaneously. It's like I
opened a gate that's been closed for a long time; and once
the gate's been opened once, it's easier to reopen it.

Charles is a broker in London. When he was a child he
had a remembrance in which he saw a former life in Mexico.
In the following account he describes a journey he took to
Mexico many years after his remembrance, and some of the
experiences he had there which convinced him that his remembrance was genuine.

I always recall a scene from my childhood. On warm
summer days I used to spend afternoons with my mother
in the garden. I was aware of much more then, as a
child, than I am now. I could see or sense a much deeper
part of life. It was as if life were a river. Since I became
an adult I have seen only the surface of the river of life;
my eyes can no longer penetrate the surface. But
when I was a child I could see beneath the surface of the
river of existence.

Anyway, one day I was with my mother in the garden.
The world around me became fuzzy; the trees, the plants,
the sky, everything became hazy, and I felt that I was in
the sky, like a bird. Scenes began to appear before me. I
was standing in the ruins of a great temple. There were
smaller temples all around me. They were mostly
covered by dense jungle. The vines grew thickly about
the trees. It was hot and humid. I could hear the sounds
of the jungle, a kind of constant music that was
punctuated by tropical bird calls. I saw a man standing
before me dressed in a ceremonial gown of some sort. He
was performing a magic rite; he was chanting an
incantation. He lifted both of his hands up and chanted
to the sky. Then he held a dish of some sort of reddish
liquid before his mouth and drank. I can still recall
every detail of the temple ruins—the broken step, the
three separate pyramidal sacrificial platforms, everything.

As a young man I was drawn to Mexico. I left home and traveled there. I spoke no Spanish and had very little money, but I was absolutely compelled to go to lower Mexico near the Yucatan Peninsula. I hiked alone for days. Occasionally I would meet Indians, but I encountered practically no one of my own race with whom I could speak. I suffered innumerable hardships and became very ill from a tropical disease. Still, something pushed me forward; I had to reach this spot which I sensed was there.

One day, almost in total delirium, I met a party of Americans who were visiting the country. They gave me some proper food, and I inquired if there were some ruins nearby that had pyramids in them. They told me of several different sets of Mayan ruins that sounded like they might fit my description, and after a brief rest I set off again. I was walking through dense jungle and mud during the rainy season, I was practically delirious with fever, I had no money and had lost sixty pounds, but still I pressed on.

I arrived several weeks later at my destination. I had visited two ruins, but neither of them was the right one. The morning of the day I found the location I had been seeking, I sensed that something particularly eventful was about to occur.

It was the exact scene I had pictured in my childhood. The ruins, the three pyramid-shaped platforms, everything except the undergrowth was the same. I stayed there for two weeks. During that time I saw much more. The story of my past was revealed in further visions I had while I was there.

I saw that I had been a priest at the temple. I had conducted sacrifices for the well-being of my people. I had led a very simple life, devoting myself totally to my work. I understood that I had come through all of the hardships on my journey so I could see where I had been before. In this sense I suppose I was directed to this spot so I could know I had been alive in an earlier

time than my life now. I would have never believed
it otherwise; it was just like I had seen it in my vision in
my mother's garden.

I saw a series of my other lives that had occurred
before my lifetime as a temple priest. I realized that
I had had hundreds of lifetimes that stretched back for
thousands of years. My lifetimes, the ones I saw, showed
me that the conception of history that man has today
is incomplete. There were four great civilizations on this
earth that we don't have records of. One of these civilizations was Atlantis. I lived in Atlantis. I saw scenes
from my life there.

Atlantis and the three other great civilizations were
destroyed in terrible wars. Their destruction was so
devastating and complete that practically no trace of them
survives on earth today. The Egyptian, Mayan, and
several other civilizations grew out of the survivors
of those great civilizations. Those few who did survive and
escaped the complete destruction went to the other
parts of the world and taught the savages as much as they
could before they too died.

The scenes of the destruction of Atlantis I have seen
were horrible. Everything was in flames. Thousands of
people were running in the streets, trying to escape.
Such powerful weapons were used that a chain reaction
in nature occurred and volcanoes erupted and earthquakes
began. The entire continent was destroyed in a nightmare
of flame and tidal waves. It was horrible.

I would have disregarded my past life visions of these
things had it not been for the accuracy of my past life
vision among the Mayans. This proved to me that I had
lived before. Had I not made the journey and if I had
only seen these things in London, I wouldn't have
accepted them as I have. This is why it was necessary
for me to make the journey there. It gave my first past
vision the verification I needed. Then I could see
and accept the rest.

EPILOGUE

The Soul selects her own Society—
Then—shuts the Door—
To her divine Majority—
Present no more—

Unmoved—she notes the Chariots—pausing—
At her low Gate—
Unmoved—an Emperor be kneeling
Upon her Mat—

I've known her—from an ample nation—
Choose One—
Then—close the Valves of her attention—
Like Stone—

Emily Dickinson

The philosophy and the experience of reincarnation are not new. The oldest civilizations on record—Egyptian, Indian, Chinese, Japanese, Tibetan, Greek and many other diverse cultures—have left clear indications that reincarnation was their accepted perspective on life. Plato himself believed in the rebirth of the soul, as have many other philosophers and mystics throughout the ages. In our modern world probably more persons subscribe to the doctrine of reincarnation than to any other single philosophy. The majority of the people in the Far East and a growing number of persons in the West view human existence as a multiple-life process. Why is it, then, that to most of us who have grown up in the West the concept of the rebirth of the soul seems so foreign? Is it simply because our Judeo-Christian orientation has provided us with only one perspective on living and dying?

191

It is my feeling that this is the case. When Moses and Christ walked the earth, they were dealing with simple agrarian peoples. It was enough for most of their followers to absorb the idea that the "Father" was in a "heaven" and that if they prayed and led a positive life, they would one day go to that heaven. These were concepts that could be understood by persons in the early stages of their spiritual evolution. Today, however, we live in a different age. On the whole, humanity is much more sophisticated. The growing interest of the West in subjects such as meditation and reincarnation indicates that we are ready to accept a fuller picture of our existence. It is in this light that I have presented the remembrances of living and dying that appear in this book—not to convince the reader that reincarnation exists, but to impart the message of hope to the hearts of persons who very much need an alternate view of existence.

Seeing scenes and events from their past was not the most important experience of my interviewees; it was their new perspective on their lives as a result of their remembrances. As a whole this group of persons had a more positive attitude toward both dying and living than any other group I have ever met. It was not simply that they had overcome their fears of death; I have met many persons who know nothing of reincarnation who are not afraid of death. It was that these individuals had come to realize not only that their lives were eternal, but that they were constantly evolving toward something better and higher. They believed in the value of life. They were able to see the problems both in their own lives and in the world in general, and instead of either running from them or idealistically believing that their problems and difficulties would simply disappear, they were actively working to make their lives better.

We live in an age of darkness and light. Never has humanity had such a capacity to create either a heaven or a hell on this planet. Those persons who have had remembrances of their past lifetimes are striving toward creating something positive both within themselves and in this world.

Personally, I do not feel that I have been "converted" to a belief in reincarnation; I do not think such a conversion is possible. But I have examined the "evidence" in as straightforward and objective a manner as is possible when dealing with such esoteric phenomena. Based on that evidence and in lieu of any other acceptable explanation for the results of this research, I must conclude that reincarnation does exist.

Nor do I feel that I have accepted a new theory. I have only taken a larger look around my world. I have explored it and questioned its structures. My only hope for the person who is reading the accounts in this book is that he will do the same. Not necessarily in the way I have, but in his own way. Wisdom means the ability to change and develop consciously, to continually question the assumptions by which we live. Had humanity not questioned the basic assumptions of its existence, we would still believe that the earth is the center of the solar system, or even that it is flat. The experiences of the persons I interviewed changed their perspective on existence just as dramatically as these discoveries changed humanity's perspective in centuries past. By reading and studying these accounts, we have shared in their experiences, and hopefully we have become wiser for our journey.

SUGGESTIONS FOR FURTHER READING

The following books have been invaluable to me in my study of the death and rebirth process. I recommend them to anyone who wishes a highly detailed explanation of the process of reincarnation.

Bhagavad-Gita. Swami Prabhavananda and Christopher Isherwood, trans. New York: Mentor Books, 1944. The principal works of Hinduism are the *Vedas, The Upanishads*, and *The Bhagavad-Gita*. Of the three, *The Bhagavad-Gita* deals most directly with the process of reincarnation. The book is in the form of a dialogue between the great spiritual master Sri Krishna and his disciple Arjuna. Sri Krishna answers Arjuna's questions on existence, the path to enlightenment, and the process of reincarnation. *The Bhagavad-Gita* is one of the cornerstones of both Hindu and Yogic thought and practice.

Death and Reincarnation. Sri Chinmoy. Published privately (1974) by Agni Press, 84–47 Parsons Blvd., Jamaica, N.Y. 11432. In my opinion, the most detailed account of the stages and complexities of the rebirth process. Sri Chinmoy is one of the leading authorities on meditation and reincarnation living in the West today. Like *The Bhagavad-Gita,* it is very readable, and even those who are relatively new to the subject of reincarnation will have no difficulty understanding the subtleties of the rebirth process dealt with throughout the book.

The Dhammapada. Juan Mascaro, trans. Great Britain: Penguin Books, 1973. The source book of Buddhism. It contains the principal teachings attributed to Gotama Buddha, who lived five hundred years before the birth of Christ. In *The Dhammapada* Buddha outlines his philosophy regarding death, rebirth, Liberation and illusion. His principles embody a way of living that will eventually lead an individual to the attainment of enlightenment and Liberation.

Life After Life. Raymond A. Moody, Jr., M.D. New York: Bantam Books Inc., 1975. Explores the phenomenon of death from the perspective of persons who have been pronounced "dead" and were later revived. The descriptions of these persons' experiences and their correlation with many of the past life accounts in this study are striking. I have benefited greatly from my reading of *Life After Life.* While the nature of our studies is radically different, I can only express my sincere admiration for Dr. Moody's continued research and for his publications on matters related to life after death.

The Summits of God Life: Samadhi and Siddhi. Sri Chinmoy. Published privately (1974) by Agni Press, 84–47 Parsons Blvd., Jamaica, N.Y. 11432. One of the few accounts of the experiences a person has in the higher stages of the rebirth process. The author deals with such topics as Samadhi, Nirvana and Bliss, Liberation and Illumination, and the Higher Planes of Consciousness.

The Tibetan Book of the Dead. W. Y. Evans-Wentz, ed. New York: Oxford University Press, 1957. An extremely esoteric text that deals with the complexities of the death and rebirth process. For a reader generally unfamiliar with the highly symbolic terminology, the *Book of the Dead* can be a trying experience. The commentaries and prefaces by Dr. Carl Jung, Lama Anagarika Govinda and Sir John Woodroffe are very valuable to the reader's overall understanding of the rebirth process and are particularly important in "translating" much of the complex terminology

Index

201

Printed in the United States
By Bookmasters